IN A

BOSNIAN TRENCH

ELVIR KULIN

WITH MAURY HIRSCHKORN

Note for Librarians: a cataloguing record for this book that includes Dewey
Decimal Classification and US Library of Congress numbers is available
from the Library and Archives of Canada. The complete cataloguing record
can be obtained from their online database at:
www.collectionscanada.ca/amicus/index-e.html
ISBN 1-4120-4884-2

TRAFFORD

Offices in Canada, USA, Ireland, UK and Spain
This book was published on-demand in cooperation with Trafford Publishing. On-demand publishing is a unique process and service of making a
book available for retail sale to the public taking advantage of on-demand
manufacturing and Internet marketing. On-demand publishing includes
promotions, retail sales, manufacturing, order fulfilment, accounting and
collecting royalties on behalf of the author.
Book sales for North America and international:
Trafford Publishing, 6E–2333 Government St.,
Victoria, BC v8t 4p4 CANADA
phone 250 383 6864 (toll-free 1 888 232 4444)
fax 250 383 6804; email to orders@trafford.com
Book sales in Europe:
Trafford Publishing (uk) Ltd., Enterprise House, Wistaston Road Business
Centre,
Wistaston Road, Crewe, Cheshire cw2 7rp UNITED KINGDOM
phone 01270 251 396 (local rate 0845 230 9601)
facsimile 01270 254 983; orders.uk@trafford.com
Order online at:
www.trafford.com/robots/04-2692.html

10 9 8 7 6

INTRODUCTION

In a Bosnian Trench is the memoir of Elvir Kulin, a Muslim Bosnian soldier, who fought for three years in the war in Bosnia. My father is indirectly responsible for this book coming into being. My father, Ralph Hirschkorn, was in the combat engineers and served in England, France, Belgium, and Germany during World War II. He was at Normandy two days after the allied invasion, in a town that was attacked by the German army during the Battle of the Bulge, and took photos of Buchenwald, a Nazi concentration camp, soon after its liberation. Because of listening to his experiences during World War II, I became interested in that war and read many books about it, particularly soldiers' memoirs. (My father died in 1989.)

When Josip Broz Tito, President of Yugoslavia, died in May 1980, I read his obituary and became interested in reading about his partisans who fought and won a guerrilla war against the German army in Yugoslavia during World War II. I read every book I could find about the Yugoslavian partisans and other Yugoslavian memoirs during that war.

I was shocked when I heard that Yugoslavia broke up in the early 1990s. I was equally shocked when I heard that the Yugoslavian National Army attacked some of its former republics and autonomous region: Slovenia, Croatia, Bosnia, and Kosovo.

After the war in Bosnia in 1996, I began to put advertisements into Sarajevian newspapers to look for pen pals and to get more information about the recent war. Many people responded to me, but most couldn't write in English, or their English was poor. An exception was Elvir Kulin. His English was excellent. He was a Muslim soldier during the 1992-1996 war in Bosnia and had interesting stories about his life during that war. He also interested me because of our similarities. Like me, he was quiet and shy and had trouble relating to his father.

After a year and a half of writing letters back and forth, I felt that Elvir's experiences during the war would make an good book. In January 2001, I visited him in Sarajevo with a tape recorder to collect more of his experiences. I took photos of him, his family, his settlement, and Sarajevo. I saw that Sarajevo is now a city of ruins, shell holes, and minefields. I took many photos of it but couldn't do its devastation justice. When I came home, I called and wrote to Elvir to get more information. I got information about Bosnian and Yugoslavian past and present history from other books, the internet, and newspaper articles. The result is this book.

This book is partly written by Elvir and partly as told to me by Elvir. It is a true story of a young, shy, sensitive Bosnian soldier trying to survive in the worst war in Europe since World War II.

All the names in this book are factual with one exception, Ferid Mozderac, Elvir's fellow soldier in Bijela kosa. The reason that Mozderac's real name was changed is because his family had properties in the town of Rudo in the Srpska Republic (the Serb Republic of Bosnia). Ferid hopes his family might be able to go back to those properties, and if the Serbs knew he fought against them, returning might be difficult. Also, Ferid admitted to having sexual relations with women while married. If his wife knew about that, she might divorce him.

Maury Hirschkorn

CONTENTS

A BRIEF HISTORY OF YUGOSLAVIA

In this book, since many references are made to past Bosnian, Serbian, and Yugoslavian history, that history needs to be told. The following is a brief history of Bosnia, Serbia, and Yugoslavia from the seventh century to 1980:

In the seventh century, two tribes called the Croats (or Croatians) and the Serbs (or Serbians) migrated and settled in territories later called Bosnia, Serbia, and Yugoslavia. Like other people in that area, the Croats and Serbs were converted to Christianity.

In 1389, the Battle of Kosovo Polje in Serbia took place between the forces of the Ottoman Empire led by Muslim Turkish Sultan Murat and an alliance of Christian forces led by Serbian Prince Lazar. Both forces suffered greatly in the battle, and Lazar and Murat were both killed. However, neither side won. The Muslim forces continued to attack and advanced through the Balkans. In 1495, the last Serbian fortress surrendered, and in 1528, the last Bosnian stronghold fell to the Ottoman Empire. Serbia and Bosnia fell to the Muslim Turks while Croatia and Slovenia (territories to the north of Bosnia) were taken over by the Hapsburg Empire whose official religion was Orthodox Christian. Because of the long Ottoman Empire occupation, many people in the area became Muslims. In Bosnia, the majority of people became Muslims.

Over the next centuries, Serbians rose against Turkish rule, but each rebellion was put down ruthlessly. In 1877, Russia declared war against the Ottoman Empire. Fighting with the Russian armies, Serbia was rewarded with its independence from the Turks in 1878.

The Hapsburg Empire conquered Bosnia and Herzegovina in 1888 and annexed it in 1908. This antagonized Serbs who regarded Bosnia as Serbian territory.

I remember another part of Yugoslavian history whenever I pass a certain bridge by tram in the center of Sarajevo. On June 28, 1914, Archduke Franz Ferdinand, heir to the Hapsburg throne and Inspector General of the Armed Forces of the Austro-Hungarian Empire and his wife were shot and killed by Gavrilo Princip, a Bosnian Serb, while driving in Sarajevo near that bridge. (A plaque at the location of the killing marks the spot.) The assassination was planned in Serbia, and the Austro-Hungarian government used it as a pretext to declare war on Serbia exactly a month later. Soon after, Austro-Hungarian troops invaded Serbia, conquering it. Germany backed Austria-Hungary, and Russia, France, and Great Britain backed Serbia. At the beginning of August 1914, World War I began.

After the war, in December 1918, Serbia, Vojvodina, Kosovo, Slovenia, Croatia, Bosnia, Montenegro, and Macedonia became the Kingdom of Serbs, Croats, and Slovenes or Yugoslavia. The king was Serbian, and the capital of Yugoslavia was in Belgrade, Serbia, and people in other areas resented that.

In April 6, 1941, Nazi Germany attacked and invaded Yugoslavia. In just a few weeks, German and Italian troops occupied all of the country. Along with Croatia, Bosnia became the "Independent State of Croatia," a Nazi puppet state, and the Ustashe (Croatian fascist soldiers) engaged in genocide against

Serbs, Jews, Gypsies, and political opponents. In reaction, Serbian peasants killed Croatians and Muslims whom they saw as collaborators.

My grandfather told me that he heard that Muslims near his village were machine-gunned and thrown into a river by Serbs. Also, he heard that Serbs tied up the arms and legs of Muslim babies and threw them against trees killing them.

Soon, two resistance groups fought the occupier: the Chetniks and the partisans. The Chetniks, under the command of Colonel Draza Mihajlovic, began to liberate areas in Serbia but were driven into Montenegro and Bosnia by superior German troops. Mihajlovic then concentrated on building up his organization and discouraged attacks against the enemy because they would provoke reprisals. Mihajlovic and the Chetniks' objective was to bring back the Serbian king, the Orthodox church, and the Serbian way of life.

The Communist partisans, under the command of Josip Broz Tito, began to liberate areas across Yugoslavia. Unlike the Chetniks, his army consisted of all nationalities of Yugoslavia, not just Serbian. Also unlike the Chetniks, he encouraged attacks against the enemy despite the reprisals. Tito's army also fought the Chetniks. Tito's objective was to make Yugoslavia a Communist country and exclude the Serbian king.

Tito moved the main partisan detachments to Bosnia, and the German army made several offenses against them. Tito was wounded in one.

At the end of World War II, with the help of British and American weapons and Russian troops, the partisans controlled Yugoslavia, and the Chetniks were defeated. 1.7 million Yugoslavs died in the war. Mihajlovic was captured, tried, and shot in 1946 as were other opponents of Tito's regime.

Russian troops occupied Eastern European countries, and they soon became Communist dictatorships. Yugoslavia became a Communist country with Josip Broz Tito as its president, but unlike the others, it wasn't controlled from Moscow.

Tito soon established a Soviet-style economic system in which all economic planning was centralized in Belgrade. He nationalized industry, commerce, trade, insurance, banking, transportation, and communications and began a rapid industrialization of the country. He used "forced labor" to accelerate the industrialization. A relative told me that immediately after World War II, people had to do difficult physical work such as building roads, constructing buildings, and working in factories without payment. If they refused, they were put into prison. Later, many Yugoslavian industries reverted to private ownership.

As in the Soviet Union and other Eastern European countries, the press in Yugoslavia was controlled by the government. Opposition newspapers were shut down, and no dissenting views were allowed to be heard.

For much of Yugoslavian recent history, the teaching and practice of religions were forbidden by the Communist authorities. Muslims were discriminated against more than other religious groups. After World War II, schools and mosques where the Koran was taught were closed down as were Muslim cultural and educational societies. That changed in 1954 when religious practices were tolerated but discouraged. However, because of past repression, many Bosnian Muslims stopped following some of the Islamic laws such as not eating pork and not drinking alcohol.

Even though Bosnia was a national republic of Yugoslavia, most of its affairs were controlled from Belgrade. Although the majority of the population was Muslim, most of the posts in the government and Communist party were occupied by Serbs. That changed slowly after Aleksandar Rankovic, Tito's Serbian secret police chief, was removed in 1966 for abusing his power.

Rankovic's police were known for oppressing non-Serbs in Vojvodina, Kosovo, and Bosnia.

Faced with nationalism especially from Croatia, Yugoslavia created a new constitution in 1974 that changed the governing system. The six national republics (Serbia, Slovenia, Croatia, Bosnia, Montenegro, and Macedonia) and the two autonomous regions of Serbia (Vojvodina and Kosovo) would be self-governing for all purposes except for foreign affairs and defense.

The President of Yugoslavia Josip Broz Tito died in May 1980. Since Tito's long time associates in the government had already died or had been removed from their offices before Tito's death, he had no successor. Therefore, a rotating presidency took over governing the country. Every few years, someone from a different republic governed Yugoslavia.

After Tito's death, the economy in Bosnia worsened partly because of the corruption of political leaders and partly because of the cutback of social programs. Those cutbacks were demanded by the International Monetary Fund and the World Bank, which loaned Yugoslavia money. It was difficult to raise children and pay for food and school. You could feel the tension in the people. Unemployment was high. Nationalist politicians, who were replacing the Communist officials, blamed the poor economy on rival ethnic and religious groups.

CHAPTER ONE

GROWING UP IN BOSNIA

As a boy growing up in Bosnia, I was not happy because my father was often drunk while the rest of the family had to bear his abusive behavior. I remember an example of this behavior that was repeated over and over again while I was growing up: It was 10 in the evening, but my father hadn't arrived home from work even though he worked the 7 a.m. to 3 p.m. shift at an import/export business. We wondered what happened to him. We waited some more, watching television until our eyes grew heavy, and we were told to go to bed. We promptly fell asleep.

We were rudely awakened by the shrill ringing of the doorbell. My mother opened the door, and my father's voice filled the flat. He was angry, demanding, and loud. He was drunk again.

"Children, come here at once!" he yelled. "I want to ask you something!"

Wiping the sleep from our eyes, my brother, sister, and I got out of our beds, stumbled out of our rooms into the hall, and stood before him. Father was an imposing figure – six feet tall and towering over us. His hands were on his hips. Near us was our mother.

"Who's the boss of this house?" he asked us.

"You are," we responded.

"Okay. Now, I want to prove what you said is true," he said. He started to command us, "Sit down! Stand up! Lie down!"

We did as ordered. I thought he would stop ordering us but was wrong.

"Sit down! Stand up! Lie down!..." he continued like a drill sergeant.

"How dare you treat them like this!" my mother yelled. "Leave them alone, and let them go to sleep!" Her face was red with anger.

He turned on her. "Why didn't you want to open the door when I rang the doorbell?"

"You know that's not true."

"Don't contradict me!" he yelled. His right arm swung at her, hitting her left shoulder with an open hand. She winced in pain. I was frightened but moved forward to defend her. But it was useless because I was a small child. My father shoved me away roughly.

People in my neighborhood used to ignore my father's behavior, but sometimes they called the militia when he got too noisy and dangerous. (The police were called the militia in those days.) As a child, I got upset when I saw someone looking at me with a smile because I thought they were laughing at my situation.

My father didn't drink every day like other alcoholics. He drank periodically, usually once every 20 days. But after each time he drank, he made the rest of the family miserable. My father drank everything that was alcoholic, but he preferred stronger drinks. His favorite was slivovitz, a local plum brandy.

Many times, I wished my father would leave us alone or die. In those days, I was sad, but my good friends, mother, twin brother, and half sister brought some joy into my unhappy life.

My name is Elvir Kulin. On February 6, 1975, my fraternal twin Amir and I were born in Bosnia. My immediate family consisted of my father Ershef Kulin, mother Ziza Kulin, older half sister Jasmina Granulo, my brother, and me. My sister was from my mother's first marriage.

We lived in Hrasnica, a settlement in the southwestern outskirts of Sarajevo. Sarajevo was the capital of Bosnia and Herzegovina (or just Bosnia), a republic of Yugoslavia. Officially, it was called the Socialist Federal Republic of Yugoslavia. The other Yugoslavian republics were Serbia, Slovenia, Croatia, Montenegro, and Macedonia. (See Map One.) Yugoslavia was an independent Communist country in southeast Europe.

Our home was a basement flat in a three-story, tan, concrete apartment building. Our flat consisted of an entry hall, a bedroom for Amir and me, my parents' bedroom, my sister's bedroom, a small bathroom, and a combination kitchen-dining room. The flat was gloomy because from its windows, we only got a view of people's legs walking by. Around our building were other apartment buildings. The apartment buildings generally looked the same; they were rectangular and three or four stories high. Most of the upper flats had terraces where the occupants would often hang their wet clothes on lines to dry. In our apartment building and the others lived the people that mostly made up Bosnia: Muslims, Serbians, Croatians, and the mixture of two of those groups. But most of us called ourselves Bosnians. There was a path from our apartment building complex to a winding road off the main street where buses stopped. Also in the path, Mount Igman could be seen in the distance.

Like the majority of people living in Bosnia, my family and I were Muslims. And like the majority of Bosnian Muslims, my family were more or less secularized. When people think of Muslims, they see people bowing and praying five times a day towards Mecca. However, with the exception of my mother, none of my family did that. To us, the main condition to being a Muslim is the belief in Allah (Arabic for God).

At a mosque, we celebrated important Muslim holidays such as Ramazan (the month when the first revelation of the Koran was made from Allah to Mohammed and is celebrated by fasting) and Bairam (the three day feast and celebration that breaks the Ramazan fast). However, we didn't fast during the whole month of Ramazon and didn't even go to a mosque regularly. My mother and sister didn't wear any covering over their heads, and we all wore Western clothes, like most Bosnian Muslims. My mother made sure we kept the Muslim custom of requiring all people to take off their shoes when entering our flat. And my father drank alcohol, which Islamic law prohibited.

Each major group (Muslims, Croatians, and Serbians) living in Bosnia and Yugoslavia, essentially spoke the same Slavic language called Serbo-Croatian and lived together with no major problems, though generally the Muslims had a better relationship with the Croats than with the Serbs. The chief differences between them were their religions. Croats are Roman Catholic, Serbs are Orthodox Christians, and Muslims are the descendants of people who were converted to Islam during the long Ottoman Empire occupation of the area.

According to the 1991 census, the population in Bosnia consisted of 44 percent Muslim, 31 percent Serbian, 17 percent Croatian, and 5.5 percent declaring themselves to be "Yugoslavian." Also according to that census, the population in Sarajevo consisted of 49 percent Muslim, 30 percent Serbian, seven percent Croatian, and 11 percent declaring themselves to be "Yugoslavian."

My family had the same last name as a famous medieval Bosnian king, and my grandfather said he heard that we might be that king's descendants, even though he had no proof. But I didn't feel as though I was descended from royalty. I had no inclination to sit on a throne, make royal degrees, or call my neighbors, "My subjects."

In 1180, Bosnia became independent of the Byzantine Empire, and King (Ban) Kulin took over the reins of power. During his 20 year rule, he improved the economy and kept Bosnia out of the many wars that plagued its neighbors. He improved relations with the King of Serbia and the ruler of Hum (later Herzegovina). Kulin's sister married the ruler of Hum. Kulin's rule was called the "Golden Age" because his country was at peace during this time.

Originally a Roman Catholic, in 1199, King Kulin, his family, and around 10,000 Bosnians became Bogomils. An offshoot of Christianity, Bogomils believed there were two Gods: a God of evil and a God of good. The God of evil created the material world and humans, and the God of good created the human soul. Bogomils denied most Catholic prayers and did not use the cross, icons, or churches. They prayed at home, made mutual confessions to each other, denied the authority of bishops, and were against the church possessing property. They taught disobedience to authority and praised poverty as a virtue. Bogomil services were guided by elders chosen by lot who read from the New Testament. Bogomilism began in Macedonia and spread to Bulgaria, Bosnia, Italy, and southern France.

Bogomilism was considered heresy to the Catholic Church, and Catholic kings persecuted them. Under pressure from Pope Innocent III and King Emmerich of Hungary, Kulin maintained Bosnian independence by recanting his conversion to the Bogomil faith.

Later, many Bogomils became Muslims.

When I was a child, my mother sometimes cleaned houses during the day. While both parents were working, Jasmina took care of Amir and me. She was responsible, but one time got careless which almost caused my brother his life. I was four. My sister, Amir, and I were home alone when our cousin Sabina ran into our flat.

"Let's go to the River Zeleznica for a swim," Sabina said.

"I'm afraid I can't," Jasmina said. "I was told not to go out. I have to take care of my brothers while our parents are at work."

"So what! We'll not be there for a long time, and your parents will not even know about it."

My sister hesitated for a moment and finally said, "We'll go but not stay there for a long time."

When we arrived, my brother and I walked along the river and threw stones into it because we couldn't swim.

"Jasmina, may I go into the water with you together?" Amir asked my sister.

"Well, I don't know. You'll have to promise to hold on to my back the whole time."

"Please take me into the water! I promise I'll do everything you say."

Jasmina noticed my disappointed face. "Don't be angry, Elvir. It will be your turn after Amir's," she said as she jumped into the water with Amir on her back.

I lay down and waited. Soon, I heard, "Help! For God's sake, help!" I jumped up, looked around but couldn't see what was happening because there were many swimmers in the water. However, I recognized my sister's voice. When I saw people gathering round a place on the bank, I ran towards them. My sister was holding my brother in her arms while he was coughing water. I felt very frightened.

The most traumatic event in the lives of all Yugoslavs was the death of Yugoslavian President Josip Broz Tito in May 1980. Tito was beloved by many people, and I saw my neighbors with tears in their eyes when they heard the news. I noticed that my parents and people in the neighborhood were worried about what would life be like without Tito. They were concerned if Tito's successors would have his wisdom and experience to run a country with different ethnic groups and religions, each wanting to assert their authority.

I was only five then and didn't know or care much about politics. I predicted there would be a huge funeral for Tito and was proven correct. On TV, I saw kings, prime ministers, presidents, and heads of government attend his services. There was a 21 gun salute. While jet fighters flew overhead, his coffin was drawn past large crowds.

According to a Bosnian Muslim death custom, when someone close to you died, you turned off the TV and put a clean piece of clothing over it. When Tito died, my parents did this to our TV for 40 days, and I was upset I couldn't watch it.

I had injured myself badly when I was six, and it was a terrible experience. I was with Amir and a group of boys from the neighborhood. With nothing to do, we made a fire behind our apartment building and kept putting trash into it. We laughed as the flames got higher. A boy named Mirko, a Serb, threw a plastic bag on the fire, and we watched in fascination as liquid plastic dropped off of it. Mirko took the bag out of the fire and swung it around. The bag flew from him and landed on my pants, which caught on fire. I yelled in pain. I tried to put out the fire but couldn't. In a panic, I ran to our building and fell down. My pants were still on fire as I screamed in pain. I felt something fall on top of me and looked up. A neighbor named

Murat covered me with a blanket, which extinguished the fire. Soon, an ambulance took me to the hospital. I had severe burns. They gave me injections and changed the bandages every two or three days. For 14 days, I was in agony.

The first time I saw a dead body was when I was seven and starting primary school. It was a summer, sunny day, and I was playing "hide-and-seek" with Amir and my friend Rudi. While Amir closed his eyes and counted to 100, Rudi and I hid behind the corner of a building nearby. Amir didn't come near us, and Rudi and I occasionally peeked to see where he was searching. Suddenly, something exploded above us, and we were momentarily deafened by the sound. We looked up and saw a burning flat on the first floor near where we were standing. We ran away and observed the burning flat from a safe distance. Amir joined us. Soon the flat above the burning one was on fire too, and people came out of the building running and coughing. Next, fireman arrived and fought the fire. Finally, a dead body was taken out, and it was so badly burnt it was almost impossible to recognize.

My best friend since childhood was a Serb named Ljubisa Dkebo. We had gone to school together and spent much of our time in the neighborhood. Sometimes, we got into trouble but not intentionally. For example, we borrowed bicycles and rode around the neighborhood. The bicycle owners, however, didn't share our love for exercise and often objected to their temporary disappearance. We also got into trouble for examining and experimenting with relatives' cars. Their owners didn't appreciate our mechanical curiosity especially when something in the car was broken. One time, our automotive interest got us yelled at by Ljubisa's father. His father's car was in his garage, and the garage door was closed. Examining the car, we turned on the ignition, and the exhaust almost suffocated us. We ran out of the garage coughing. Another childhood friend of mine was a Muslim named Almir Advic. I first met Almir through other friends. Because he was fun to be with, I spent more time with him than with other people, even Ljubisa Dkebo. Gradually, Almir and I became the best of friends. Because he was a year older than I, we didn't go to school together. However, we were together at other times in the neighborhood. Almir often got into trouble and liked to play practical jokes on people. People sometimes got angry at him, but not too much because in the beginning, it was just Almir having fun. He also played practical jokes on me.

I was a quiet, shy person. However, in Almir's presence, my behavior changed. I become loud, behaved badly, and played tricks on people. At first, the tricks were harmless. We hid people's belongings and laughed while they looked for them. Then we returned them. Later, we told people false stories such as their car was on fire or a relative was in the hospital. After they ran out to their car or called their families, we laughed and told them it was a joke. Finally, we sent phony calls to the police and fire department that there was a fire in a neighbor's flat when there wasn't.

I followed Almir's behavior because he was a strong personality, and the destructive behavior was a way to vent my anger against my father. However, because of the troubles he got me into, I stayed friends with Almir but stopped participating in his pranks.

Because the educational system in Yugoslavian schools was better than Iraq, the Iraqi government sent some students here to study, mostly at military academies. In 1982, Jasmina met such a student, a Muslim named Osama Shaghati. He was from the city of Basra and studied agronomy in Sarajevo. (Osama's brother studied at a military academy in Serbia.) Later that year, Jasmina and Osama got married.

Because Muslim men from the Middle East were known for treating their wives rudely and not as equals, Jasmina knew our mother wouldn't approve of the marriage. Therefore, she and Osama were married in secret. When my mother found out about the marriage, she became angry at Jasmina and tried to convince her to end it. When Jasmina refused, she didn't talk to her for a few months.

It was two or three years after Jasmina married that I finally met Osama, and then it wasn't planned. I asked her to go somewhere with the family. She said she couldn't because she had to go somewhere else. She said her husband was waiting for her, and she had to leave with him. I walked with her and met him. Osama was sitting in a green car. He was short, had dark curly hair and had darker skin than most Bosnians. When he told me his last name, I thought about how strange sounding it was. We spoke briefly, and they left. I wished I had a better first meeting with my brother-in-law. I wanted to know more about him.

Jasmina and Osama owned and ran a grocery store in Alipasino polje in the western part of Sarajevo. She named the store "Osama" after her husband. However, "osama" is also the Bosnian word for "loneliness," and that name caused questions and amusement from customers. Later, I worked as a shop assistant for "Osama" for several years, as did my brother, before the war forced it to close down.

I once asked Osama what life was like in Basra.

"It's a large city in southern Iraq on the Tigris River," he said. "There are many buildings, factories, and oil wells there."

"Tell me more about it."

"The climate is hotter than here. Basra isn't covered with desert as other areas in Iraq are. It has many trees."

I decided not to ask Osama about the political situation in

Iraq or about the wars fought there, and he never volunteered that information. He just said sometimes he felt homesick. Later, when I heard about the bombing of Basra, I guessed that Osama was glad he wasn't there. (During Iraq's three recent wars, Basra was shelled and bombed by the Iranians, the Americans, the British, and the insurgents fighting British occupation troops.) It didn't surprise me that Osama didn't want to return to Basra and Iraq.

When I was 15, I graduated from primary school and went to commercial secondary school. My grades were average. What interested me most was studying English. Unlike Western Europe, English was not mandatory in all schools in Yugoslavia. However, English was mandatory at my school in Hrasnica, and I got good grades in it. Being an English teacher was a highly paid, attractive position, and there weren't many English interpreters. My goal was to go to college and get a degree to be an English school teacher or an English translator and interpreter. I considered myself to be a shy, quiet person but capable when teaching children and adults.

My first English teacher was a middle aged woman named Vesna Divac, a Serb. She was competent, her knowledge of English was good, and she was a perfectionist when it came to correct English pronunciation. However, she was also overbearing, loud, inconsiderate, had an unpredictable temper, and gave slaps to the cheeks of students who didn't know their lessons. Her breath sometimes smelled of alcohol. She liked me and was pleased with my performance, but in her presence, I felt fear and was mostly quiet.

Vesna asked other students to go mountaineering with her on Mount Igman. Frightened, they declined. I also declined except for one time. As she bounded up the mountain, I got tired halfway and lagged behind her. She reached the top and waited for me. As we ate our lunch, Vesna questioned me about my future. "You're the best student in my class. Your written and spoken English is excellent. Do you plan to continue it?"

"Yes, I do."

"You should. The knowledge of English is very advantageous."

I had already decided to make learning English a priority.

Despite my shyness, I was somewhat popular in secondary school. I had many friends. Some girls were also interested in me, and some of those wanted to have sex with me. I didn't understand the reason for the girls' interest. Maybe it was because I was so mysterious. I was said to be "a very complicated but interesting crossword puzzle" because I didn't talk about myself more than was necessary.

CHAPTER TWO

YUGOSLAVIA'S CIVIL WAR BEGINS

Yugoslavia's war against itself began when Slobodan Milosevic, a Serbian nationalist, gained power. In 1986, Milosevic became head of the League of Communists of Yugoslavia, and in May 1989, he was elected president of Serbia. In July 1989, to mark the 600th anniversary of the battle at Kosovo Polje between Serbian and Muslims troops, he organized exhumations of the Serbs who died there and had funerals for them.

In the fourteenth century, Ottoman Muslim Turkish troops led by Sultan Murat invaded Serbia and fought Christian troops led by a Serbian Prince Lazar. In 1389, those troops fought each other in Kosovo Polje in Serbia. That battle led to Serbia and Bosnia being occupied by Turkish troops and being part of the Ottoman Empire.

Milosevic made a speech at the site of that ancient battle. He said how Serbs had always suffered, and it was time for them to wake up and unite to defend themselves from the Muslims, Albanians, Croatians, and Slovenians.

Milosevic seemed to be suggesting that Muslims had all the powerful positions in Bosnia, and the Serbs had none and were being oppressed. We knew it wasn't true. Even though Muslims

19

were a majority in Bosnia, most people having influential positions such as generals, doctors, and teachers were Serbs.

After listening to his speech, my mother and I looked at each other in dismay.

"What's this guy talking about?" I asked. "Is he comparing a battle that happened in 1389 to the situation today?"

"He's stirring up trouble."

"Why?"

"To help his political position. Son, with this guy as ruler of Serbia, we're in trouble."

Many Serbs thought differently. I heard that some of them compared Milosevic to Jesus Christ, and many Orthodox Christian priests were on his side.

Milosevic's nationalistic speeches continued as did Serbian nationalist programs on Yugoslavian TV. Many of my Serbian friends and schoolmates were influenced by them. They no longer thought of themselves as Bosnians but as Serbs. Their behavior changed in different ways. For example, Serbo-Croatian (or Bosnian) is written in Latin and Cyrillic. Muslim Bosnians mostly wrote it in Latin, and Serbian Bosnians mostly wrote it in Cyrillic. Before, many of my Serbian friends preferred to write it in Latin because the letters were easier to write than Cyrillic. Now, because of the nationalism, they went back to writing it only in Cyrillic and said I should write it in Cyrillic too because it was a superior alphabet.

Serbs laughed at some Muslim religious practices too. "What's with you Muslims being called to prayer several times a day and bowing towards Mecca?" they asked. "What a silly, primitive custom."

Serbia had two autonomous regions: Kosovo and Vojvodina. In March 1989, Milosevic and the Serbian Assembly removed the political autonomy of those regions. Their affairs would now be directly controlled from Serbia. This brought demonstrations and strikes in Kosovo, which were put down by the Serbian security police.

In 1990, Alija Izetbegovic, a Bosnian Muslim leader, was elected president of Bosnia, defeating Radovan Karadzic, a Bosnian Serb nationalist. (Izetbegovic was the only president of a Yugoslavian republic who wasn't a former Communist.) The Serbian controlled press and Karadzic suggested that because of Izetbegovic's past, he would make Bosnia an Islamic fundamentalist state and persecute Serbs just as Muslims did 600 years ago. A document Izetbegovic wrote called the Islamic Declaration was used as proof of this.

As in other cases, the Serbian press distorted Izetbegovic's past. He spent two years in prison from 1946 for organizing the "Young Muslims," which defended Muslims against attacks by the Communist authorities. He later graduated from law school at the Sarajevo University. He became a legal consultant and director of a building company. The Islamic Declaration released in 1970 was a general treatise calling for general Islamic renewal. It didn't even mention Bosnia or Yugoslavia. In 1983, Izetbegovic and 11 others were charged with "hostile and counter-revolutionary acts derived from Muslim nationalism," and the Islamic Declaration was cited as evidence. They were all found guilty and went to prison from 1983 to 1989. In 1990, Izetbegovic became the leader of the Party of Democratic Action, which represented Bosnia's Muslims.

Our Serbian neighbor Tomo believed everything the media said about Izetbegovic and constantly railed against him to my mother. They had loud, angry arguments.

"Izetbegovic wants to make Bosnia an Islamic state and oppress all the Serbs in that state!" Tomo yelled at her.

"That's all lies spread by the Serbian media and Milosevic!" she yelled back. "Milosevic wants to create conflicts between

21

different groups to keep himself in power! The longer he stays president of Serbia, the worse the situation will be for all Yugoslavians, not just the Serbs!"

"You're wrong! Milosevic is a great man, and he'll make Yugoslavia a great country! Izetbegovic is an evil man, but Milosevic will get rid of him."

Even if Izetbegovic wanted Bosnia to become an Islamic fundamentalist state as the Serbian press claimed, most Muslim Bosnians would not welcome that state. We would have huge demonstrations in front of government buildings until Izetbegovic resigned.

In the middle of these major political changes, my school principal decided to have class trips to Belgrade, the capital of Serbia. By bus, I went with teachers, my brother, and other students. As we entered Serbia, I wasn't impressed with the countryside. It was flat, and there were few trees around.

Belgrade was as boring and dull as the land around it. Most of the buildings were gray and lifeless. The city was crowded, and most of the Serbs we heard talking seemed snobbish and crude. They cursed too much. I didn't like it. We went to parks, zoos, and shops. We saw Tito's grave. A group of stiff, unsmiling soldiers were guarding it. The way they were marching back and forth, they looked like guard dogs. The grave site was called the "Flowerhouse" because it had many flowers around it.

"Ariana, please sing a Bosnian folk song," Mirko said to Ariana as a group of us walked in a square in the center of Belgrade. (Most Bosnians enjoy singing.)

"You want me to sing in the middle of all these people?" Ariana asked.

"Why not?" Mirko asked. "Let's bring some cheer to these dull Belgraders."

Other students also wanted Ariana to sing, and she finally agreed.

Ariana sang a popular folk song. Encouraged, she sang other songs. One of the songs started like this:

"A young man played his lute.

Its strings were like a girl's hair.

Its neck was like an eagle's feather…"

People walking by looked at her but didn't stop.

After Ariana finished, we heard applause from a young Yugoslavian soldier standing off to the side. He approached us.

"Bravo! Bravo! What kind of songs are those?" he asked. He sounded Serbian.

"They're Bosnian folk songs," Ariana answered.

"They're excellent. Are you all from Bosnia?"

"Yes, we're students visiting," someone else said. We introduced ourselves.

"Excellent. I hope you Muslims enjoy your sightseeing trip through Belgrade. There's a lot to see here…"

"I'm not a Muslim," Mirko interrupted. "I'm a Bosnian Serb."

The soldier stared at Mirko for a moment. He seemed confused. "How could it be possible you're a Serb and living in Bosnia?" he asked. "You should be living in Serbia."

"There are many Serbs in Bosnia," I said.

"There shouldn't be. Serbs should stay together in Serbia and not live under the Muslims…"

After a few minutes of arguing where Serbs should live, the soldier changed the subject and turned to Ariana. "If you like singing, Ariana, there's a concert near here," he said. "Why don't you go with me there tonight?"

"I can't leave my friends," she said.

"We'll go another day then," he said.

"We're leaving Belgrade soon. I can't go on a date with you."

"Tell me what life is like in the army," Mirko asked the soldier, trying to change the subject. "I'll be mobilized soon and wonder about it."

"Serving in the army is quite boring. I could use some excitement…"

Finally, we left Serbia. I wasn't impressed by the city or the people or the political system there.

My father and I had constant arguments. The worst occurred in 1991. He came home drunk again and yelled at my mother and her mother, who was visiting.

"What kind of a fuckin' wife are you?" he yelled. "Your cooking is terrible! You can't keep the house clean! You're worthless!"

My mother kept quiet as Amir and I listened from our room. The next day, my father sobered up and complained to my mother about pains in his stomach and legs. She seemed to be worried, and the sympathetic look on her face made me furious. When she was alone with me, I confronted her.

"Why are you so concerned about him and taking care of him when yesterday he kept cursing at you?" I asked.

"He's your father, and he's not feeling well."

"His sickness is just withdrawal symptoms from the drinking! He's a bastard! He doesn't deserve help from you! He deserves someone to knock him to the ground!"

My father heard my yelling and came into the room.

"What's with the yelling around here?" he asked.

I was still scared of him. But I had grown almost as tall as he and decided to make a stand. I got close to him. "I want you to stop cursing at my mother!"

"Or what?!"

"Or I'll kill you!"

He picked up an ashtray and held it over me. I picked up something heavy nearby and held it over him.

"Go ahead. Hit me with that ashtray!" I yelled. "It will be the last thing you'll do! It will give me an excuse to kill you so I won't go to jail!"

He continued to hold the ashtray.

"Go ahead you bastard! Hit me!"

He knew I was serious and didn't move. But he didn't back down either. My mother got in the middle of us and pushed us away from each other.

"Stop!" she yelled. "They'll be no fighting or killing in this house!"

My father seemed relieved that she stopped the argument from escalating to blows. He knew I wasn't a small child anymore and could cause him serious injury. He put down the ashtray and left the flat.

Milosevic refused to allow the next rotating president of Yugoslavia to assume power and changed the status of Yugoslavia's republics. Slovenia, Croatia, Bosnia, Montenegro, and Macedonia would no longer be self-governing but ruled directly from Belgrade. The leaders of Slovenia, Croatia, and Macedonia rejected that status and, encouraged by the leaders of Germany, declared their independence. This was first accepted by Germany and then by the European Union, the United States, and other countries. Yugoslavia would now consist only of the republics of Serbia and Montenegro.

Milosevic said he would allow those former republics to become independent states, but "Serbian" territory in those states had to become part of Serbia. Since Croatians, Muslims, Slovenians, and other Yugoslavian people also lived in "Serbian" territory, the states rejected that demand. Milosevic then sent the Yugoslavian military (called the Yugoslavian National Army or the JNA) backed by Serbian paramilitary forces to invade and occupy that "Serbian" territory.

Slovenia declared its independence on June 25, 1991. The next day, Yugoslavian tanks and soldiers attacked Slovenian territory, and the newly formed Slovenian army counterattacked. This was later called the "Ten Day War," in which the Yugoslavian army was defeated and withdrew from Slovenia.

Croatian President and nationalist Franjo Tudjman declared the independence of Croatia on the same day that Slovenia did. Unlike Slovenia, there was a large Serbian population in Croatia, and many Serbs were formed into paramilitary units, which Milosevic armed.

Together with Yugoslavian tanks and troops, they began to attack and occupy Croatian territory in August 1991. The Croatian army unsuccessfully counterattacked. The war was notable for the destruction of the eastern Croatian city of Vukovar and the shelling by land and sea of the Croatian port city of Dubrovnik.

On TV, my mother and I watched a news program on Yutel about the fighting in Vukovar. (Yutel was a Yugoslavian TV station, and its name was a contraction of the words, "Yugoslavia" and "television.") The Yugoslavian military laid siege to Vukovar for three months before it surrendered in November 1991. Almost every building in the city was destroyed. There were thousands of Croatian refugees, and hundreds of people killed were buried in mass graves. Yutel reported that Croatian troops were torturing and attacking innocent Serbs there, and the Serbs were fighting back. Because the Yugoslavian army began the attack, we had doubts that Yutel was giving us the full story.

As we stared at the ruins of Vukovar in amazement, I felt sorry for the Croat refugees and Serbs who died in the fighting.

I couldn't understand how Yugoslavian people could destroy their own city and kill each other.

In December 1991, Serbian paramilitaries and the Yugoslavian army occupied 30 percent of Croatia, in territory called the Krajina. In January 1992, a cease-fire was declared. UN troops were sent to the Krajina to maintain the cease-fire, but people felt their presence was to prevent Croatian troops from taking back their territory.

Macedonia declared its independence on September 1991, and UN troops were sent there to discourage the Yugoslavian army from attacking. But Milosevic showed no interest in Macedonia, and no attacks on that territory took place.

People were afraid that Milosevic would attack Bosnia next and hoped a war could be avoided. However by the fall of 1991, Yugoslavian tanks, artillery, and soldiers started to be moved from Croatia to the outskirts of Bosnian cities and towns including Sarajevo, and by the winter of 1991, the Bosnian government applied to the European Union for recognition as an independent state. All sides were heading for war.

On the Serbian government-controlled TV, I saw stories about Muslim atrocities against the Serbs and "proof" that Izetbegovic and other Muslims wanted to make Bosnia an Islamic fundamentalist country in which Serbs would be attacked and killed. The Serbian people were being propagandized for war against the Muslims.

At the start of 1992, the most brutal war in Europe since World War II was about to begin, and I would be in the middle of it, first as a civilian and then as a soldier.

CHAPTER THREE

THE WAR COMES TO BOSNIA

Milosevic and Serbia took a position similar to Hitler and Germany, and Tudjman and Croatia took a position similar to Stalin and the Soviet Union. Hitler and Stalin were enemies but agreed to attack and carve up Poland during World War II. Milosevic and Tudjman were enemies but agreed to attack and carve up Bosnia during this war. Izbetbegovic took a position similar to Neville Chamberlain's when he tried to stop the war through negotiation and compromise. Fearful of provoking Serbia, he didn't build up his army and even surrendered Bosnian weapons to the Yugoslavian army. While he did this, Yugoslavian and Croatian armies prepared to attack Bosnian cities. The Yugoslavian army distributed weapons to Bosnian Serb paramilitaries, and the Croatian army distributed weapons to Bosnian Croat paramilitaries.

With the Yugoslavian and Croatian army blocking the roads, no food or other supplies were able to get into Sarajevo. People were uncertain how long that condition would last and lined up at grocery stores, including my sister's, and bought almost everything in sight. Jasmina, Osama, and I didn't have a moment's rest ringing up and packing customers' orders at the store. At the end of the day, we tried to decide what to do.

"We're running short of many items – sugar, flour, dairy items, and canned goods," Osama said. "All of those things are being snatched up."

He was right. I saw a lot of empty spaces on shelves that had been fully stocked and in the refrigerated sections.

"I think it might be a good idea if we take some things home for ourselves," Jasmina added.

That's what we did. Jasmina also thought the conflict would end soon and suggested we should keep some food in the store for when it opened again. We did as she requested.

We brought food home until it filled our refrigerator and cabinets. The store stayed open, and people continued to line up.

On February 29 and March 1, 1992, there was a referendum on whether Bosnia should be an independent country. Radovan Karadzic urged Serbs to boycott the referendum and prevented voting in some places. The Yugoslavian air force dropped leaflets over Bosnia also urging Serbs not to vote. I picked up a leaflet, but it didn't interest me. It didn't seem to have anything to do with me.

I was only 17 years old and couldn't vote. I saw crowds going to the voting stations. At "Osama," and in our apartment building, I heard many people talk about the vote. Most Muslims and Croatians wanted independence, and most Serbians didn't. People knew the Yugoslavian army was in Bosnia, and war might break out, but they didn't know exactly when.

"Bosnia will suffer if we become independent," said Tomo, our Serbian neighbor. "We have to become part of Serbia."

"I don't agree with you," I said. "Bosnia has resources, minerals, mines, and farms. We don't need Serbia."

"If Bosnia votes for independence, we'll be destroyed. The Yugoslavian army is already in Bosnia. It's very powerful.

They've been collecting weapons for fifty years. Most of the generals in the Yugoslavian army are Serbian, and the power is in Serbian hands."

I kept silent. I knew the Bosnian people didn't have enough weapons to fight the Yugoslavian army.

On March 2, the results of the referendum were announced. Officials said 63.4 percent of the eligible voters participated in the referendum, and 99.43 percent voted for Bosnian independence. A day later, the government of Bosnia declared the republic's independence.

After the declaration was announced, Bosnian Serb paramilitaries attempted a coup in Sarajevo. They set up barricades and sniper positions near government buildings. They also had barricades throughout Sarajevo and its outskirts to remove weapons the Muslims acquired. Muslims demonstrated against their actions.

When I went to work, I noticed the barricades and saw many people protesting. I also saw that some people had smashed shop windows and stolen merchandise.

Because the trams and buses weren't running, I took a taxi home. In the center of Ilidza, (a Sarajevian settlement north of Hrasnica) there was a barricade with paramilitaries around it. They were armed, uniformed, and wore white bands on their arms. They stopped everyone who tried to pass. As we approached the barricade and stopped, a tall policeman with fair hair approached us.

"Show me your documents," he asked the taxi driver and me in a polite way. We did so.

He looked at the documents and handed them back to us.

"Get out of the car," he said, and we did.

He searched us, and the other police looked through the car. They were looking for weapons but didn't find any. I recognized him. He was a Serb. His name was Nebojcha, and he lived in my neighborhood. I decided not to talk to him. Finally, they let us go.

When I got home, I told my mother about my experience.

"Amir is coming home with a lot of groceries," she said. "I hope they don't give him trouble."

When Amir finally got home, the expression on his face told me he had had problems.

"After we were stopped at the barricade, they told us to get out of the car," he said, his words racing. He was obviously still agitated. "They searched us and searched the car, but that wasn't enough. They grabbed the bags of food and emptied the contents on the street. I've never felt more humiliated."

"What did you do?" I asked.

"What could I do? They were armed, and I wasn't. However, I did manage to pick up some food from the ground."

"At least you're not hurt, and that's what counts," my mother said. "When you're unarmed and surrounded by armed men, it's not the time to try to be a hero."

Soon after, Muslims and Croatians set up barricades across Sarajevo to disarm the Serbs. I had to pass some of these barricades. Neighbors recognized me and didn't search me, but strangers did.

We heard that the Yugoslavian army occupied Visegrad, a city in the east of Bosnia on the border of Serbia. On TV, my mother and I watched a quarrel between Yugoslavian General Milutin Kukanjac and Murat Sabanovic, a citizen of Visegrad.

"What the hell is your army doing in Visegrad, mother fucker?!" Sabanovic yelled.

"Calm down! You're wrong if you think the Yugoslavian army is here to kill people. The troops are sent to keep peace in that town."

"So why are they shooting at the people of Visegrad at this moment, while we're just talking?!"

"Don't worry. I'll immediately give the troops the order to stop firing in that area."

"If you don't order them to retreat at once, I'll blow up the hydroelectric power station!"

"No, don't do that! Believe me. Everything will be okay..."

The story was that Murat Sabanovic, a Muslim militia leader, and some of his soldiers seized the Visegrad Dam. They threatened to blow it up and send a flood of water rushing down the Drina River back to Serbia unless Yugoslavian troops withdrew from Visegrad. People knew that Sabanovic was knowledgeable about explosives because 10 months before, he blew up a statue of Ivo Andric, a Serbian Prize-winning novelist. Eventually, Sabanovic didn't blow up the dam. After a week stand-off, his men opened two spillways in it, sending a large amount of water into the river. That damaged some structures along the river.

Even though the country was in a serious political situation, I simply couldn't accept the fact it could turn into a war. For God's sake, we were all were citizens of the same country, the former Yugoslavia.

I felt bored watching TV and decided to go long distance cycling to Vrelo Bosne, an attractive town northwest of Hrasnica.

I had to pass a barricade manned by Serbian paramilitaries, but they didn't provoke me. They were nice and allowed me to pass.

When I arrived at Vrelo Bosne, I saw a UN vehicle surrounded by armed UN soldiers. They wore blue helmets. Some of them were jogging.

UN troops called UNPROFOR or the UN Protection Force arrived in Sarajevo on February 21, 1992, but their presence was not related to Bosnia. They were to keep the cease-fire between Croatia and Serbia after their war, and their headquarters was in Sarajevo, seen as neutral ground.

I felt good seeing them. They would stop the war from getting worse, I was sure.

After cycling some more, I stopped to rest at a lake where there were lots of swans and ducks. It was marvelous to watch them gliding on the water's surface. Looking at them, I could forget what was happening in my country.

"There are more guns than members of my family in my house." The voice of a middle aged woman interrupted the silence I was enjoying so much. She was dressed in black and had a Montenegrin accent. (The Montenegrins were allies of the Serbians.) There were two more women with her, carrying cans of something in their arms, and they seemed happy about the events that were occurring.

On my way home, I had to get off my bicycle because there was a steep hill ahead, and I wasn't strong enough to climb it. Walking the bike, I saw a man with a long, blue coat carrying an automatic rifle approach me from a cottage.

"Stop! Stop!" he yelled.

I ignored him. I felt intense fear and wanted to get away. My hands shook, and my legs felt wobbly. I was about to get on my bicycle when he aimed his gun at me.

"Don't move, and come here at once, or I'll shoot!" he yelled. I could tell he was a Serb, and I did as ordered.

"Why didn't you stop the first time I ordered you?" he asked.

"Believe me, if I heard you, I certainly would've done what you wanted." I didn't know what to say except to lie.

With his fist, he hit me in my face so hard that I fell. I was in pain.

After a few minutes of lying on the ground, I heard him order me to stand up and lean against the wall of the cottage with my face towards it and my arms high above my head. I did as ordered and felt his hands touching my body all over. He was looking for something.

"Is this a gun?" he asked with his hands on my pants pocket.

"No, it isn't. I'm only seventeen and don't know how to use a gun." Tension made my voice sound strained.

"The fact you're so young doesn't necessarily mean you don't know how to shoot."

"Believe me. It's only a pack of cigarettes. I don't like guns."

He put his hands in my pocket and took the cigarettes out.

"How come such a young person smokes cigarettes?" he said. "May I take one?"

"Please take all the cigarettes I have, and let me go home. My mother will be worried if I don't come home soon."

"Okay, but before I let you go home, I'll give you a piece of advice."

He aimed his rifle at me and ordered me to lie down. He put a knife against my neck and asked, "What would happen if I cut you here?" He had a strange look on his face, and I felt so frightened that I couldn't talk. It seemed as if he was hesitating about whether to kill me or not.

"If you want to kill me, please do it with your gun," I said, crying.

"No, I don't want to kill you at all. I want you to realize what a fool you were when you came here alone. You know, people are so nervous these days, and somebody could hurt you. Believe me, I didn't want to kill you at all. I want to show you how generous the Serbs really are. My son, go and tell the truth about us to your people." (To the Muslims, he meant.)

I got on my bicycle and rode away. There were no words to describe how happy I was at that moment. I felt like a person born again. I was still trembling though when I stopped at the

UN vehicle and spoke to the soldiers. If that Serb followed me, I wanted their protection. The soldiers looked at me strangely, surprised that a Bosnian would suddenly stop and talk to them about nothing important. Fortunately, I didn't see the Serb and rode away.

What made that guy decide not to kill me? I still don't know. There is a saying in Bosnia: "You can't run away from destiny." Maybe it wasn't my destiny to die on that day.

The Serbian coup failed, and most Bosnian Serbs left Sarajevo and Hrasnica for Bosnian areas that the Yugoslavian army controlled. Muslim refugees from other towns and cities in Bosnia moved into their flats. In one such flat near us, a Muslim family turned on the oven, and something in it exploded. The police examined it and discovered hidden in the oven were bullets which exploded. Hand grenades were also in the oven but fortunately didn't explode. The former owner of the apartment was a Serb named Sreto Ivezic, and he had moved to the town of Kalinovik. He and I used the same entrance of the building. Ivezic didn't take the weapons with him because Muslims found a gun on him at a barricade and took it, and he was afraid to try to take the bullets and grenades also.

One of Serbs who left was Ljubisa Dkebo, my childhood friend. Ljubisa showed up at my flat to say goodbye. "My father wants us to leave," he said. "He said if we stay here, the Muslims will kill us. My brother said that will not happen and wants us to stay. They had terrible arguments. But my father is the head of the house, and it looks like we'll leave."

"What do you want to do?" I asked.

"I want to stay, but if my family leaves, I'll go with them. Do you remember how we ignored politics when we hung out together? I guess we can't ignore it anymore."

"Where are you going to go?"

"My father wants to go to the place in Bosnia where there's

a Serbian majority. We might go to Pilava. My dad was born there. We might go to Reljevo. My mom was born there, and we have relatives there. We'll see."

We wished each other the best, and he left. I hoped that Ljubisa wouldn't be ordered to join the Bosnian Serb paramilitaries and shoot at Muslim Bosnians. I never saw or heard from him again despite requests to the Red Cross after the war.

On April 5, there was a huge peace demonstration in Sarajevo. I didn't join it because I wasn't interested in politics then. My mother and I watched it on television. We saw many protesters, and most were working people. Some had the flag of the ex-Yugoslavia, and some were carrying photos of Tito. Most of the people were cheering "Bosnia! Bosnia!" While they were doing that, we saw someone shoot from a hotel in the central part of Sarajevo. Some people were shouting, while most of them lay down immediately. Then the crowd got angry and ran towards the Vrbanja Bridge. There was more shooting, and we saw blood on the street.

"Son, do you see what those bastards are doing to us?" my mother said.

"Yes, I don't see how it's possible for people to shoot at peaceful protesters. Who's shooting? Is it the army of Yugoslavia or the Serbs? I don't understand politics."

"The army of Yugoslavia and the Serbs are the same. They're not human. They deserve to be killed but not with a gun. They must suffer."

I kept silent.

Later, we heard that 10 protesters were wounded by Serbian gunfire, and on the Vrbanja Bridge, Suada Dilberovic, a female medical student from Dubrovnik, Croatia, was killed. She became officially the first person to die in the war. After the war, the name of that bridge was changed to the Suada Dilberovic Bridge.

The next day, two of our Serbian neighbors Milka Krvavac and Tomo visited our flat. Milka was divorced and lived with her daughter. Most of the time, she was friendly. However this time, like Tomo, she argued with my mother about whether those protesters provoked the Yugoslavian army into shooting at them.

Milka also argued against the separation of Serbia and Bosnia. "I can't imagine Bosnia without Serbia!" she yelled. "Bosnia will die if it becomes separated from Serbia!"

Using tanks, rocket-propelled grenades, and automatic rifles, the Yugoslavian army and Serbian paramilitaries attacked the Sarajevian Police Academy in Grbavica (a southern district of Sarajevo). My mother was upset because a relative named Suad Paleta was a student at that academy. She spent most of the day watching the television to try to get information. We didn't know who was killed or wounded and were worried. Eventually, the Serbs captured the academy.

On April 6, 1992, the European Union recognized Bosnia as an independent state. In front of the Holiday Inn, Serbs opened fire on more protesters, killing five of them. That day, President Izetbegovic announced the war and called people to register to join the Bosnian army. My father went to register and came home soon.

"I joined the army and am supposed to join the anti-terrorist force," he said. "Their job is to guard buildings with guns. My company is closed down, and they don't need me." (He worked as a clerk for "Forwerding," an international company that provided transportation for imported goods.)

"I would like to volunteer," he said to my mother. "Do you mind if I go?"

"No, go if you want," my mother said without emotion.

"What will happen to you and the children?"

"Don't worry."

He turned to me. "Listen to your mother, Elvir. Don't dare disobey her. Do everything she says."

"Okay, I'll obey her." Then he left.

To be honest, I felt happy that he left. We didn't get along, and I didn't enjoy his company. I hoped he would have many "terrorists" to fight and would be away for a long time.

Just before the war started, my father stopped his drinking and some of his insulting behavior. However, I didn't love him as a son should love his father and was angry for what he had done in the past. I don't know why he stopped drinking when he did, but I have ideas. When the war started, alcohol was difficult to get. Also, many people were armed during the war, and if a drunken person insulted them, the drunk would often get shot.

Later that day, someone knocked on the door. I opened it and saw it was Suad Paleta. As he came into the flat, my mother, brother, and I stared at him. We couldn't believe he wasn't killed or wounded when the army attacked the police academy.

All of us shouted at once, "Are you alive?!"

Suad sat down and with a trembling voice told us his story of how he survived the attack on the academy.

Suad's parents lived in Gorazde, a city southeast of Sarajevo. All communication with Gorazde was disrupted, and he couldn't get back there because the Yugoslavian army blocked the way. Therefore, my mother decided that Suad would stay in our flat for as long as he could.

Suad was a good house mate. He helped the family as much as he could.

On April 7, the United States recognized Bosnia as an independent state. This was followed by Bosnia being recognized internationally.

While walking in the neighborhood, I ran into Almir Advic, my Muslim childhood friend. With a smile on his face, Almir said he was responding to the call by our president to volunteer to join the army.

"You're too young," I said. "You're only seventeen. Why don't you wait until you receive the mobilization order when you become eighteen? That will be soon."

"Perhaps by then, the war might be over. I want to get into the action right away. Now seems to be the time to attack the Serbs, and I'll be glad to help push them back to Serbia," he said. "What about you, Elvir? Are you going to volunteer to join the army?"

"I thought about that, but my mother probably wouldn't let me. I'll wait for the mobilization order when I become eighteen. There's no rush."

I wished Almir luck, and he left.

We heard on television that Karadzic had declared a Bosnian Serb republic and called it the Srpska Republic. The Yugoslavian army and Serbian paramilitaries seized 70 percent of Bosnia including the cities and towns of Visegrad, Zvornik, Foca, Banja Luka, Pale, Prijedor, Bijeljina, and Rogatica to become part of that republic. Karadzic became president of the Srpska Republic, and his headquarters was in Pale, a small town only 12 miles southeast from Sarajevo. Banja Luka, a city northwest of Sarajevo, was designated as the capital of the Srpska Republic.

Muslims in the Srpska Republic were "ethnically cleansed," meaning the removal of a specific civilian population according to their ethnicity. The removal took the forms of killing, being put into detention camps, or expulsion.

Hrasnica became a collection center for survivors of those "ethnically cleansed" areas, and refugees found shelter in any space available. Many people who now lived in my apartment building were refugees from areas controlled by the Serbs. I spoke to some of them and heard the same story of Serbian paramilitaries killing Muslims and burning their homes. I tried to understand the actions of the Serbs. It seemed like weapons, and the authority to use them, turned ordinary people with jobs and families into murdering monsters.

At the same time, the Croatian army (in Croatian: Hrvatska Vojska or HV) and Bosnian Croat paramilitaries called the Croatia Council of Defense (in Croatian: Hravatsko Vijece Odbrane or HVO) attacked and occupied Bosnian territories near the border of Croatia. The commander of the HVO was Mate Boban, a Croatian nationalist, and their headquarters was in Kiseljak, located only 15 miles west of Sarajevo.

In Sarajevo, the Yugoslavian army occupied Ilidza (with the towns around it) and Grbavica. They tried to occupy other sections of Sarajevo but were stopped by Bosnian soldiers and other armed groups. During the fighting, I heard gunfire. They also occupied the hills and mountains surrounding Sarajevo except for Mount Igman. (Mount Igman was a mountain that started southwest of Sarajevo and continued to the west.) So the Yugoslavian army surrounded Sarajevo on three sides.

The Bosnian Serb paramilitaries in our war named themselves Chetniks after the Chetniks who fought and were defeated by the partisans during World War II. The word Chetnik was previously used by Serbian guerrillas who fought troops from the Ottoman Empire and Austro-Hungarian Empire. The aims of the current Chetniks were the same as the past Chetniks, though their actions were different. They wanted to create a Serbian state. Many Chetniks in our war dressed like Chetniks did in the past, with uniforms, white armbands, and beards. To us, a Chetnik was a Serbian who tried to harm other people who didn't belong to the Serbian nationality.

Chapter Four

THE SHELLING BEGINS

From their positions in Ilidza and Grbavica and in the hills and mountains surrounding the city, the Yugoslavian army began shelling Sarajevo on April 21 with different calibers of artillery and mortars, mostly 60, 81, and 82 millimeter shells. We heard distant explosions. Hrasnica's turn would come soon.

While walking near my apartment building, I heard alarms. People scrambled to their homes, and I ran home too. Then I heard shells exploding. I should have felt scared, but I didn't. Instead I felt amused because to my surprise, the shells sounded different from those in the war films I had watched when younger. In the films, the shells whistled followed by an explosion. In Hrasnica, the shells sometimes whistled and sometimes didn't. (Usually, a shell didn't whistle when it landed near you.) Also, when the explosions were near, I smelled powder and felt a gust of warm air.

When I walked into the entrance of my apartment building, a neighbor directed me to the shelter in the basement where other people were staying. They were sitting on chairs and crates. This room wasn't near any outside walls and was considered to be the safest place in the building. I saw my mother and brother sitting. They looked at me without speaking, and silently I sat down next to them. We heard another explosion and then another.

I looked around and saw many of my neighbors including Tomo, Milka Krvavac, and Milka's daughter. Tomo looked terrified. He was shaking and crying. Each time a shell exploded, he jumped. He wasn't praising the "great Yugoslavian army" now.

Sitting in the crowded shelter upset me. I needed room and was getting restless. "I'm going upstairs," I said and stood up. "I want to see what's happening outside."

"Are you crazy?! You're staying here until the shelling stops!" my mother commanded.

I sat down. Finally the shelling ceased, and it became quiet. We went into our flat. After 10 minutes, the shelling began again, and we again went into the shelter. After a few minutes, the shelling stopped.

The next morning, I walked through the streets and saw the awful damage – shell holes, damaged buildings, glass in the street, and damaged cars. I heard about some of our neighbors who were killed and wounded. I also heard that other neighbors were leaving for other countries and other former republics of Yugoslavia.

The next day, we again heard the sound of whistling and explosions as more artillery and mortars crashed into our settlement.

The shelling was too much for Tomo. Soon, he left for an area controlled by the Yugoslavian army. Milka and her daughter stayed in Hrasnica.

On most days, the explosions of shells were constant sounds in Hrasnica. Their targets seemed to be residential and outdoor shopping areas, not military installations. In most cases, the Yugoslavian army shelled for a few minutes, stopped for a few minutes, and then shelled again. In that way, they could kill and wound people who thought the shelling had ended and had left their shelters.

Many people died because they didn't understand what a shell could do. They thought that a shell had to hit you directly to kill you. They didn't know that a shell had shrapnel, which could travel far from where the shell exploded.

The shelling was worse on the weekends because Serbs got off from work then. Besides stealing Muslim property, some Serbian civilians spent their weekends shelling Sarajevo with the Yugoslavian army.

In the latter part of 1993 and after, most people no longer stayed in the shelters during the shelling, including my family and myself. They stayed in their flats. I don't know if the reason was because they were brave or because they were tired of going into their shelters all the time.

The main way to go from Hrasnica to Sarajevo was to go north to Ilidza and east to Sarajevo. Another way was to go south through Mount Igman and go north. Because the Yugoslavian army occupied Ilidza and the mountains south of Sarajevo, the only way now to get to and from Sarajevo was to go over the tarmac of the Butmir Airport. (See Map Two.) It was through the airport that my sister reached us.

Jasmina's grocery store "Osama" finally closed down. The Yugoslavian army still blocked the roads, so they couldn't get more supplies. She and her husband lived in a flat in Dobrinja, a settlement in the southwest part of Sarajevo. Now she came home, and when I saw tears in Jasmina's eyes, I thought that the Yugoslavian army had done something to her or to her husband. I was wrong.

"I left my husband," she announced to my mother, brother and me.

"What happened?" my mother asked.

"He has a girlfriend named Edina who lives near our store in Alpasino polje. Neighbors told me about her, and I discovered them. I suspected something was going on before but refused to believe it because Osama was such a nice, gentle person who would do anything for me."

When Osama admitted to having this girlfriend, my sister left him. My mother decided that Jasmina would stay in her old room, which she did. I felt angry at Osama for hurting my sister. If he wanted to date women, he shouldn't have gotten married. Nobody forced him.

I didn't understand Osama. While other Sarajevians were worried about how they would survive in the city under constant siege, he was having fun with a woman behind his wife's back.

Jasmina also told me that Dobrinja was shelled, and some of her neighbors were killed and wounded by shells and gunfire. It seemed that the Yugoslavian army was shelling all the areas of Sarajevo they didn't conquer.

An embargo was introduced by the UN in September 1991 against Yugoslavia, and even though Bosnia wasn't part of Yugoslavia now, the embargo wasn't removed against it. Yugoslavia had huge amounts of weapons stockpiled and seized weapon factories in Bosnia. When the embargo began, the Yugoslavian army had hundreds of tanks and artillery pieces while the Bosnian army had only two tanks and a small number of artillery pieces. Therefore, the Yugoslavian army could send shell after shell into Sarajevo while the Bosnian army could hardly respond. Later, the Bosnian army got weapons from other countries, but it was never enough.

As shells continued to land in Sarajevo, we expected the UN to send more troops into Bosnia to help us. But they didn't. Haris Silajdzic, the Bosnian foreign minister, asked Boutros

45

Boutros-Ghali, the UN secretary general, to bring more UN troops into Bosnia. Instead, some UN troops were removed because of the danger. I still saw UN troops and had an encounter with a UN soldier when I went to smoke cigarettes. I had started smoking earlier in the year. Of course, I didn't want my mother to know about it so I hid while making and smoking them. During a lull in the shelling, I bought some tobacco and went to a sidewalk next to a wall to roll it into cigarettes. I noticed a UN vehicle in the street and saw a UN soldier jump out of it and approach me.

"What do you have there?" he said. "It looks like drugs." He sounded British.

"No, it's Bosnian tobacco," I said in English "I'm rolling it into cigarettes."

"You speak English. What you're holding looks like drugs to me."

I felt uneasy because I knew a drug possession charge could land me in prison. I was also angry at this soldier. A city was being attacked and destroyed in front of him, and he was worried about drugs.

"It's not drugs," I said.

"I think it is drugs, and I'll give you three packages of cigarettes for it."

I felt relieved. I thought he wanted to arrest me for drug possession, but he just wanted to buy drugs. I traded the tobacco for the cigarettes and ran home.

Soon, my mother found out about my smoking. When she entered my room, she smelled them.

"Are you smoking?" she asked me.

I finally admitted I was. "My friends were smoking and offered me one. I couldn't say no."

"You call that an excuse! You're to stop smoking immediately!"

"You and dad both smoke."

"That doesn't make it right for you to smoke! You're only seventeen! That's too young! You must stop smoking immediately! Do you understand me?!"

"I understand."

I tried to stop, but the craving was too strong, and I smoked again. My mother eventually found out about it and accepted it. "I'm partly to blame," she said. "I set a poor example by being a smoker." Soon, my brother also took up the habit, making all of my family smokers.

One of our new neighbors was an older man who recently moved into a flat vacated by a Serbian family. We sometimes said "Hello." to each other at the entrance to our building. He was tall, wide-shouldered with black and gray hair and in his early forties.

"Hello, my name is Ibro," he finally said. After I introduced myself, he said he had a son also named Elvir. I thought our conversation wouldn't last long, but I was wrong. He was nice to talk to and had an interesting life.

In spite of Ibro being poor, he had had a happy childhood. He had been a construction worker in Croatia until the war there began. Then he volunteered to join the Croatian army and fought in their war. He left the Croatian army in April 1992 in order to volunteer for the Bosnian army. He didn't say much about his experiences in the Croatian army except to say it was terrible.

"Some soldiers in my unit called themselves the Ustashe and took delight in killing Serbian civilians," he said. (The Ustashe were Croatian fascist soldiers during World War II.) "I didn't approve, but I was one soldier and could do nothing." (During the 1991 war between Serbia and Croatia, both sides took part in "ethnic cleansing." Serbian troops "cleansed" Croatian civilians, and Croatian troops "cleansed" Serbian civilians.)

Ibro also gave me advice about the shelling. "Elvir, when you hear a shell falling or a gun firing, don't try to run away. Lie on the ground, and try to get behind something." I remembered his advice.

A year or so after we last talked, I heard that Ibro was killed in the battle of Gornji Vakuf, his native town. Located in western Bosnia, Gornji Vakuf's population was half Croatian and half Muslim. In 1993, the town changed hands many times between the Croatian and Bosnian paramilitaries, and most of the buildings were damaged. It was ironic that Ibro was killed by the army he had served with two years earlier.

Besides artillery and mortars, the Yugoslavian army also attacked Hrasnica with katyushas. (The katyushas were multiple, explosive rockets first used by the Soviets against the Nazis during World War II.) We heard them wail across the sky and heard explosions.

I was lying in bed at night and heard a katyusha followed by a crash that sounded near. I jumped out of bed and got dressed. The noise woke other people also. I ran out of the building down the courtyard to a neighboring building. A top corner flat was on fire, and I could feel the heat. Many people were around, and firemen were trying to put the fire out. I went home after watching for a while.

In the morning, we got details about what happened to that building. A woman was in her flat taking a bath. When the katyusha hit, the hot water tank fell on her and injured her. Firemen said the tank kept other debris from falling on her and saved her life. (In Bosnia, people get hot water from a tank located on the shower wall above them. Just before they take a shower, they turn the tank heater on.)

As shells continued to fall on Hrasnica, Jasmina seemed to be preoccupied with something else. Something was troubling her. Finally, she spoke to my mother and me, "I've been getting many calls from Osama. He apologized, promised not to see that woman again and wants me to come back to him. What do you think I should do?"

We kept silent. Finally, my mother spoke. "You know I was against this marriage from the beginning and tried to get you to end it a long time ago. But how do you feel about it? Do you still love him? Do you forgive him?"

"I don't know. I'm angry for what he did and shouldn't go back to him. However, we had good times together, and I miss his company. I think I'll give him another chance."

The next day, my sister crossed the airport again and went back to Dobrinja.

The telephones stopped working in Hrasnica, except in the flats of high Bosnian officers. Therefore, we couldn't contact my sister to find out what was happening with her after she left. Also, letters delivered through the Red Cross didn't reach their destinations, so we couldn't contact her that way either. We finally got information about my sister from an unexpected source. Two men knocked at our door. When my mother answered it, they spoke to her in English. Since she couldn't understand them, she called for me to translate.

They said they were humanitarian aid workers and had news about my sister and her husband. We invited them in and gave them ersatz coffee, which was made from wheat. Real coffee wasn't available for civilians during the war. Even though they spoke in English, neither was from American or England. One was from Egypt, and the other was from Jordan. Both had dark complexions.

"In Dobrinja, we met your sister and her husband," one

of them said. "Because the telephones aren't working and you might be worried about her, your sister asked us to give you a message from her. The message is that she and her husband are okay, and you shouldn't worry about them."

As I translated for my mother, I noticed the men had strange expressions on their faces.

I became confused. What was going on with these men? Did they know a secret about Osama?

"Your sister and her husband are short of wood, so we brought them wood over the airport," the other said.

"Thank you for helping my daughter and her husband," my mother said after I translated the sentence.

"It's nothing," the first one said. "We came to Bosnia to help people suffering in the war. Your sister and her husband needed help, so we helped them."

"We're only sorry we can't help more people," the second one said.

The men briefly spoke about their humanitarian aid work and left. It seemed that Jasmina and Osama got extra attention from these men because Osama and they spoke the same language, Arabic.

I never saw those men again and never discovered the reason for their strange expressions.

I was sitting in our flat when I heard the whistle of a shell and an explosion in front of my building. Someone shouted for help. I ran outside and saw three wounded people. There was a man dressed in blue jeans and a green T-shirt lying behind a hedge. Not far from him was a man on the opposite side of the courtyard with his back leaning against the wall of a cafe. In front of the building next to my building was a young girl about eight. I thought at first that the man behind the hedge was my brother because he was tall and wearing a T-shirt. When

I looked closely at his face, I thanked God that he wasn't my brother but Rusid, a neighbor. I shouldn't have felt happy, but I did. He was wounded and bleeding badly from his back and legs.

"Neighbor, please help me," Rusid said.

I hesitated whether to help him or the girl first and finally decided to help the girl.

"Please be patient until I've helped the girl," I said to Rusid.

Her name was Karolina, and she was also a neighbor. She was wounded in her stomach, not bleeding badly, conscious, and was laughing because of shock. My friends Suke and Sedin and my brother joined me, and we brought the girl into the building to give her first aid.

We saw other people helping Rusid, so we went to the other man. He was also from the neighborhood, and his surname was Viteskic. He was wounded badly in his chest. I saw the inside of his body and saw his lungs move. Our bandages were too small to cover the wound, so someone got a blanket. As we tried to put the blanket on the wound, a geyser of blood jumped out and hit me in the face and arms. We put the blanket over the wound and carried him into the building. I took his legs. They were slippery like a fish because of the blood. As we moved him, I heard drops of blood hitting the sidewalk, and I smelled the blood. As we reached the building and put him down, he died in our arms.

Soon an ambulance came and took the three people away.

Later, we heard that Karolina also died, and Rusid became an invalid. His spine was damaged. He's paralyzed and in a wheelchair for life.

Seeing Viteskic die in front of me was terrible. How many other dead and dying people would I would see in this war?

Because we shared our food supply with neighbors who didn't have much, we ran out faster than expected and had to wait on line for it. Some food came from aid organizations, and some came from people who brought it over via Mount Igman. The usual favorite Bosnian dishes were pies. There was burek (a layered meat pie), sirnica (cheese pie), and zeljanica (spinach pie). We also liked cevapcici (lamb and beef rolls rolled into a bread), chicken dishes, soups, and all kinds of vegetables. In ordinary times, we drank sour milk, coffee, and wines. Now, only beans, bread, potatoes, water, and ersatz coffee were available.

On TV, we heard that the Yugoslavian army captured Bosnian President Izetbegovic. He arrived by airplane at the Butmir Airport and didn't know that the Yugoslavian army had just seized it. When he got out of the airplane, Yugoslavian soldiers grabbed him.

One of Izetbegovic's aides was interviewed. "When the president didn't arrive, I called the airport to find out what happened, and to my surprise, President Izetbegovic picked up the phone," she said.

"Oh, my God! Oh, my God!" my mother shouted "The monsters kidnapped our president!"

"I'm sure they'll kill him," I said.

"I'll pray to Allah to save him."

On Yugoslavian General Kukanjac's orders, Izetbegovic was taken to a Yugoslavian barracks in Lukavica, and we expected him to be killed at any moment. But the Bosnian army, Yugoslavian army, UN representatives, and Bosnian Vice President Ejup Ganic reached a deal. Before the war, the Yugoslavian army had army bases throughout Yugoslavia's republics. After Izetbegovic's capture, two such bases in Sarajevo were surrounded and attacked by Bosnian army units. Despite attempts, those 200 soldiers were unable to escape the Bosnian encirclement. The arrangement reached was that Izetbegovic would be freed, and Bosnian soldiers would safely escort those Yugoslavian soldiers out of the city.

Izetbegovic was freed after a day of captivity, and Kukanjac and UN vehicles escorted the soldiers out of the city in a column of 20 trucks. However, witnesses reported that some of the fleeing Yugoslavian soldiers were shot at, some were killed, and some had their trucks and weapons seized by Bosnian soldiers. Kukanjac escaped from Sarajevo but was soon dismissed by Milosevic, along with 40 other Yugoslavian officers.

Even though we were glad that Izetbegovic survived, we knew he was unable to lift the UN embargo or get UN troops to help us fight the Serbs. The war continued.

CHAPTER FIVE

THE CHETNIKS TAKE OVER

Serbian, Muslim, and Croatian leaders agreed to a 21 day cease-fire during which the Yugoslavian army would withdraw from Bosnia. The UN officials arranged the agreement after a string of truces failed. There were several truces during the war, as Yugoslavian troops moved to better positions, collected their wounded and then began the shooting again. Also, more UN troops were sent to Bosnia.

We were skeptical of the Yugoslavian withdrawal and were proven correct. The Chetnik army, under the command of General Radko Mladic, occupied Yugoslavian army positions and manned their tanks and artillery pieces left behind. The Yugoslavian government also continually sent supplies to the Chetniks, and Serbian "volunteer" soldiers from Yugoslavia joined them.

Soon, the Chetniks began the shelling of Sarajevo again. Their favorite targets were people waiting in line for food. Chetnik snipers also shot at Sarajevian people from rooftops, holes in the sides of buildings, and mountainsides. They also shelled Hrasnica, and I again heard the sounds of whistling followed by explosions. In May 1992, an average of 16 people a day were killed in Sarajevo.

The Chetniks also shelled and damaged historical buildings in Sarajevo, such as the National and University Library, the Sarajevo Oriental Museum and the National Museum.

Oslobodjenje (Liberation) was the only Sarajevian newspaper to run throughout the war. It functioned in the basement of its building when the top floors were shelled repeatedly and destroyed by Chetnik artillery.

At a bakery on Vase Miskin Street, the only bakery open in Sarajevo, a mortar shell exploded in the middle of a crowd waiting for bread. At least 20 people died immediately, and around 100 were wounded, many of them badly. Later, the total went to 30 killed. On TV, we saw the street and sidewalk covered with blood and smashed bodies.

"Oh, my God. Oh, my God." my mother yelled, and she cried.

"How could they target people waiting on line for bread?" I asked.

"They're no longer human."

Then my mother thought of something else. "I know your sister sometimes goes to that bakery," she said. "I have to call their flat and find out where she is."

The telephones were working this time, and with a shaking hand, my mother called Jasmina's flat and spoke to Osama. Jasmina wasn't in, and Osama didn't know where she was and if she had gone to that bakery. My mother was upset by his lack of knowledge.

A few hours later, my sister telephoned us and spoke to my mother. After she hung up, she told me about my sister. "She saw the long line on Miskin Street and decided to look for food at some other place. Thank God. Thank God."

There were distant explosions to the east. Unlike the explosions in Hrasnica, these went on day and night without stopping. Using tanks, artillery, mortars, and rocket-propelled grenades, the Chetniks went on the offensive against the Sarajevian settlement of Dobrinja. They set some buildings on fire and shot at people trying to escape. Other civilians were killed as they waited on line for food and water. Most of the people killed were usually buried in graves next to their apartment buildings because it was too dangerous to bring them to the cemetery.

The Chetniks surrounded and took sections of Dobrinja, but the Bosnian army resisted, often shooting rocket-propelled grenades at their tanks. The Chetniks then destroyed parts of the settlement they couldn't capture. Since my sister and her husband lived in a flat in Dobrinja, we were worried but couldn't get through by telephone.

On TV, we saw the settlement under attack. In the flats the Serbs captured, they killed some civilians and took others to Kula. (Kula was a prison in the Serb-controlled Sarajevian settlement of Lukavica that was known for torturing and killing people.) Also, many refugees left the settlement, and some of them said the streets were filled with corpses.

"Oh my God! Oh my God!" my mother cried as she watched the TV.

Finally, Jasmina telephoned us and spoke to my mother. "What's happening?... Where are you?... Calm down, it will stop... What are you going to do?..." I heard my mother say.

After my mother hung up the telephone, she yelled, "Oh God! My daughter!"

"What did Jasmina say?" I asked.

"She said that Dobrinja was being bombed, buildings near her were burning, and she was frightened. I tried to calm her down. She said there were Chetnik soldiers in the flat opposite hers, and they were shooting through her windows into her flat. She had to crawl through the flat to pick up something."

Days passed, and the fighting continued. The telephone rang, I picked it up, and it was my sister again.

"How are you?" I asked.

"Somehow I'm alive. Yesterday, someone knocked on the door, I looked through the peephole and saw a soldier wearing a Yugoslavian uniform. I didn't open the door and was afraid he would shoot through it. Then I heard my neighbor, a woman, open her door and speak to the man. He wanted to take my husband and me to Kula prison. The neighbor told the soldier we were good people, a nice couple and convinced him to go away."

Jasmina asked where our mother was, and I told her she was out. But I promised to tell her what Jasmina said.

I prayed to God that the shooting would stop and felt helpless I couldn't do anything. My prayers were answered. The Chetniks were defeated in Dobrinja and withdrew from most of the settlement. However, a large part of Dobrinja was destroyed. The parks in Dobrinja were filled with graves of the victims of the shooting.

We again couldn't get through to my sister by telephone and feared the worst. Finally, she called us. Their flat in Dobrinja was badly damaged. They had left after the fighting, were unhurt, and now living in a flat with friends in Dzidzikovac in northern Sarajevo. We were very happy to get that news.

The United Nations Security Council demanded that the Serbs end their fighting, put their heavy guns under United Nations control and threatened military force for non-compliance. The Serbs refused. This was followed by the arrival of President Francois Mitterrand of France in Sarajevo who met with Izetbegovic and Karadzic. A day after Mitterrand left, we heard about an agreement they had reached. Serbian troops would withdraw from the Butmir Airport, and 850 UNPROFOR troops would take their place. Those UN troops' objective was the same as in Croatia: to protect food and medicine convoys and to protect citizens in cities called "safe areas" from attack. Sarajevo was a "safe area," as was Srebrenica, Gorazde, Zepa, Tuzla, and Bihac. However, when the Serbs attacked "safe areas," UN troops did not return fire. Since the UN was supposed to be neutral, their orders were not to take sides in the conflict. They could only defend themselves when attacked.

Part of the agreement was that UN troops wouldn't let Muslims cross the airport's tarmac. The Butmir Airport was only to be used to deliver food and medicine to Sarajevo.

We were glad the Chetniks no longer controlled the airport but wished that UN troops would help us break the Serbian siege.

Even though Serbian troops no longer held the airport, they still occupied other areas around Sarajevo and let us know it. Their artillery continued to shell Sarajevo and Hrasnica. Again, the sounds of explosions filled our days and nights.

The leaders of the seven major industrial countries said they would support UN military action to get aid to areas in Bosnia. This was followed by an appeal by Izetbegovic to US President George Bush to attack the Serbian forces and supply the Bosnian army with arms and ammunition. Izetbegovic met with Bush in Helsinki, Finland. Bush vowed to keep food and medicine going to Bosnia but rejected the appeal for military intervention.

Why was the United States was doing nothing while the Serbs were slaughtering the Muslim population of Bosnia? Perhaps President Bush was waiting for the Serbs to conquer all of Bosnia, and there wouldn't be a need for America to be involved. We heard that America didn't want to get involved in another Vietnam. During World War II, Serbians were excellent guerilla fighters against the Nazis. But this was not World War II or Vietnam.

Only two years before, another Muslim country was attacked; in August 1990, the Iraqi military invaded and occupied its neighbor to the southeast, Kuwait. The UN prevented Iraq from trading with other countries, but that wasn't sufficient for President Bush. He imposed a naval blockage against Iraq and sent over a half million troops to Saudi Arabia, on the border of Iraq and Kuwait. Those US troops were joined by coalition troops from countries around the world. In January 1991, US and coalition troops began the bombing of Iraqi military forces in Iraq and Kuwait. This was followed by an assault against the Iraqi military in February 1991 using tanks, artillery, armored vehicles, helicopters, warplanes, soldiers, and marines. The Iraqi military quickly surrendered to coalition forces in mass numbers and withdrew from Kuwait.

How could the U.S. rush to help Kuwait when it was under attack but ignore Bosnia when it was under attack? Perhaps it was because of the abundance of oil in Kuwait and the lack of oil in Bosnia.

My family and friends agreed that if the U.S. and the UN couldn't assist us militarily, they should end the embargo against Bosnia, so we could defend ourselves.

In June, I met my old friend Almir Advic on the street during a lull in the shelling. It was good to see him. He looked thinner, didn't wear a uniform but had the same smile on his face. As he was about to talk, we heard whistles and explosions nearby. People around us ran to their shelters.

"Let's get off the street!" Almir yelled.

We saw a bombed out building and ran into it. Almir smiled again and was full of stories of his experiences at the front.

"We're holding our positions, and the Chetniks are holding

their positions," he said. "We're under constant gunfire and have had casualties."

"Did your unit try to push the Chetniks away from Hrasnica?" I asked.

"Yes, but it's difficult to attack them because our brigade doesn't have enough weapons and ammunition, and the Chetniks seem to have an unlimited supply of weapons and ammunition. They also have tanks. It's a bad situation."

Finally, the explosions and our conversation ended, and we separated.

Soon after, I heard the sad news that Almir was killed in battle. Our forces wanted to conquer a position the Chetniks held near Hrasnica, but after heavy shelling, our unit retreated. Near a factory owned by the "Famos" company, Almir fell, and our forces weren't able to recover his body. (Before the war, "Famos" owned four factories in Hrasnica that produced tank, truck, and car parts. During the war, the Chetniks destroyed this factory after removing its equipment.) Later, our troops exchanged bodies with the Chetniks, and Almir was brought back. He was killed by a small piece of shrapnel, and at first, they couldn't find the wound.

Because funeral processions at graveyards were often shelled by the Chetniks, many people were buried between two and three in the morning, as was Almir. I didn't go to his funeral or any funeral during the war because I didn't want to be shelled. However, I'll always remember Almir and will miss him. Goodbye my friend.

To mark the 100th day of the Sarajevian siege, the Serbs dynamited the four power transmission stations around Sarajevo. The hospitals had emergency generators, but the rest of the city was plunged into darkness. Sarajevo's main nursing home also had an emergency generator, but the building had been destroyed earlier. The next day, electricity was restored to the Sarajevo army headquarters, the main telephone switching station, and government buildings. But there was no electricity for the rest of the population.

Because of shelling, Hrasnica also lost electricity, and the conveniences we took for granted disappeared. We had no lights, no TV, and no radio. I kept turning switches on out of habit, but to my frustration and anger nothing happened. It was humiliating. We used candles and often walked through our flat in darkness, bumping into furniture. The electric stove didn't work, so we had to cut down trees, gather wood, and cook on a wood stove we shared with neighbors.

In Sarajevo, electric pumps that provided water weren't functioning, so residents had to find a pipe or spring, wait on line, and fill up containers with water. In Hrasnica, we still had water for now, but the telephones weren't working.

With the Chetniks' withdrawal from the Butmir Airport months earlier, that again became the only way for people to either escape from the city or to bring food from the countryside into the city. Even though UN troops tried to prevent it, many people crossed over its tarmac. Since the area around the airport was flat and had no trees, the people became clear targets for Serbian gunners who shot at them. People then crossed the airport at night. However, when UN troops heard a noise on the airport's tarmac in the dark, they shone spotlights on the people, and Serbian gunners shot at them again.

My mother approached Amir and me with a serious look. "Boys, when I last spoke to Jasmina, she said the flat they're living in was very crowded, and I spoke to them about living in our flat. Also, I read their area is being shelled severely. Go to their flat in Dzidzikovac, and bring them here."

We had heard about the many people who were killed trying to cross the airport and were apprehensive.

"Do they want to live here?" I asked her.

"I spoke to them about that. Unfortunately, I can't speak to them now because the telephones aren't working. So you'll talk to them."

"Can't they cross the airport without us?" Amir asked.

"Enough excuses!" she yelled. "Boys, go to Dzidzikovac! Get your sister and her husband, and bring them here!" She gave us their address.

We decided to cross the airport at night. We would run swiftly across its tarmac and drop to the ground if a spotlight shone on us.

We walked through the settlement of Butmir and reached the airport between 8 p.m. and 9 p.m. UN soldiers were there, and each time we tried to cross the tarmac, they sent us back. I told them we had to get our sister and her husband, but they didn't listen. They said that only UN personnel were allowed in the area.

It wasn't until dawn that we finally crossed. Except for gunshots in the distance, it was quiet. Fortunately, nobody shot at us or shone lights on us, and we reached Dobrinja safely.

Because transportation wasn't available, we had to walk through Sarajevo to reach the settlement of Dzidzikovac. Destruction was everywhere. Buildings were destroyed, and I saw mortar holes on the streets, sidewalks, and the sides of buildings. As in Hrasnica, people looked nervous. They walked on the sidewalks but ran across the streets to keep from getting shot. We did the same. Barricades were constructed all over, and blankets were strung out in many exposed sections to block the view of the Chetnik snipers. Frequently, we heard explosions and rifle shots.

After three hours of walking, we saw a vehicle on rails that looked like a small tram. It was traveling in the direction we wanted to go, so we jumped into it. After 15 minutes, we arrived near our destination.

When we arrived at their flat, Jasmina and Osama looked at us with surprised expressions.

"What are you two doing here?!" Jasmina yelled.

"Mother sent us to bring you both back to live with us in Hrasnica," I said. "She heard about the crowded conditions you're living in and wants to help."

"It's terrible here," Jasmina said. "We live on top of each other. There's no privacy. I'll pack our belongings, and…"

"I'm not going," Osama interrupted. "I heard that 800 to 900 people were killed crossing the airport, and I don't want to join them." (Actually, the number of people killed was lower than that. In the first four months of people crossing the airport, 60 were killed.)

"My mother told us…" I started to say.

"I don't care what your mother said!" Osama yelled. "She's not my mother! I'm not crossing the airport!"

"Maybe the reason you don't want to go is that you'll not be able to see your girlfriend!" I yelled.

"That's between my wife and me! That's none of your business!"

"You hurt my sister, so it is my business!"

"Do you not want to live in my mother's flat because you're angry at her?" Jasmina asked.

"No, I just don't want to be killed. This is not my war. The Serbs aren't my enemy."

"You're a Muslim, and that makes you the Serbs' enemy!" I yelled.

"I'm not crossing the airport!"

"What are you going to do?" Amir asked. "Stay here?"

"No, I'm going to find some other way to get out of Sarajevo and find a place where there's no fighting. Then we'll talk about us staying there, Jasmina."

"That's fine," Jasmina said. "You can do that. But I'm leaving with my brothers to Hrasnica, with or without you."

At 6 p.m., the three of us left. This time, we didn't see any trams and walked the whole way back.

People saw where we were heading, advised us to be careful, and asked about the war.

"When do you think the war will end?" one of them asked.

"I don't know," I answered "It seems to be going on forever."

A woman with her five-year-old son also saw where we were going and asked to walk with us. We agreed.

"I also want to cross the airport but don't know the best way to get there," she said. "I'm afraid of getting too close to the Serbian positions."

The woman said she was from the town of Breza in central Bosnia. They left during the fighting and came to Sarajevo because she thought it would be safe. But with all the shelling, shooting, and little food, she had decided to leave.

"Where will you go when you leave Sarajevo?" Amir asked the woman.

"I don't know. Maybe we'll go back to Breza or anywhere where there's no shooting."

"Once you get to Hrasnica, maybe you could get transportation to the west," I said.

"How do I do that?"

"There are aid agencies in Hrasnica. One of them might help you. I could contact one of them for you."

"I would really appreciate that," she said. "Could my son and I go with you to Hrasnica and sleep at your flat for a day? We're both exhausted."

Surprised at the request, Amir, Jasmina, and I looked at each other. We didn't know this woman.

"We'll have to ask our mother, but I'm sure it will be okay," Jasmina said. "You can sleep at our flat."

"Thank you so much," she said.

"Thank you," the boy mumbled.

Between 10 p.m. and 11 p.m., we reached the airport. As before, each time we tried to cross the tarmac, UN soldiers sent us back. Bosnian soldiers arrived. They wanted to get ammunition across the airport, and UN soldiers wouldn't let them. They had a loud argument. More UN soldiers joined the fray. With the UN troops' attention elsewhere, it looked like a good time to try to cross again.

Other people got the same idea, and a large group of men and women ran across the tarmac, and we ran behind them. We heard a loud noise. A spotlight was turned on, and it moved towards us. The light illuminated some of the group, and we heard machine gun fire from the Chetniks. Then the Chetniks mortared us, and we saw explosions around the group and people falling down.

"They're shelling us!" I yelled to Amir and Jasmina. "Get down! Get down!"

I looked for a place to hide, saw a ditch, and jumped into it. There was water in it, and I got soaked. The spotlight passed over me, and the shooting and shelling stopped.

I heard moaning. Some of the people were injured. I looked over the ditch and saw UN troops walking away from the wounded people. They were ignoring them. I didn't see the woman from Breza, but I saw her son. "Help! My mother's on the ground!" he cried. "She's hurt!" A Bosnian man picked the boy up and carried him back to Dobrinja. "Help my mother! Don't leave her!" the child screamed.

A UN soldier appeared in front of me, grabbed the back of my shirt, picked me up, and rudely shoved me.

"What are you doing?!" I shouted as I shoved him back.

He pushed his rifle into my chest and yelled at me in English with a British accent, "Do you want to die?!" Other UN soldiers joined him. Amir ran to us and explained to the soldier in Bosnian that we wanted to return to our hometown. He didn't understand, so I repeated our request in English. After hearing me, he paused for a moment and slowly pointed his finger towards Hrasnica. "Get bloody lost!" he yelled. We walked to the other side of the airport where my sister joined us. She looked pale and frightened.

Finally, we arrived in Hrasnica, and Jasmina moved back into her room. We told our mother about our terrible experiences crossing the airport's tarmac.

"Oh my God. You'll never cross that airport again," she said. "At least, you're safe, and the family is back together." She didn't seem surprised in not seeing Osama. "Whenever he wants to come, he's welcome."

The electricity was working again for a short time, and the next day on TV, we heard about the attack we had witnessed at the airport. 11 Bosnians were killed, and others were wounded.

With a shaking voice, Jasmina told us about her experiences during the attack on Dobrinja. "The Chetniks came with tanks and artillery, and the Bosnian army and Dobrinjan citizens tried to stop them," she said. "Osama and I constantly heard the sounds of explosions. I saw a column of Chetnik tanks come down a street. A man hiding in an alley shot a rocket-propelled grenade at the lead tank and blew it up. Another tank shot a shell at him, and he disappeared in an explosion. After the smoke cleared, I saw the remains of what was left of him. He was in pieces. His legs were on one side of the alley, and his arms were on another side. People outside were shot down, so Osama and I stayed in our flat and hoped a shell wouldn't find us. The Chetniks controlled the building across the street from us, and the Bosnian army controlled our building. The Chetniks kept shooting through our windows, so we had to crawl on the floor. We had to keep our flat door unlocked so that Bosnian soldiers could enter. A few times, Bosnian soldiers came into our flat, shot rocket-propelled grenades at the Chetniks and quickly left, so that when the Chetniks shot back, they wouldn't be there. But Osama and I were there with the bullets flying above us."

Suad Paleta decided to go back to his family in Gorazde. In our flat, he told my family about his decision.

"Why?" my mother asked.

"My home and family are in Gorazde, and I belong there. I want to thank you for letting me live here for so long. Tomorrow at midnight, I'll leave."

"You'll have to go over mountains and through forests that the Chetniks occupy," my mother said. "It's very dangerous."

"I know. I have experience going over mountains, and I'll hide if the Chetniks come near me."

"Will you join the army when you get to Gorazde?" my mother asked.

"Yes, if they can use me," he said. "I was already trained to use weapons at the police academy. I can't sit back and do nothing while the Serbs slaughter us."

We wished Suad luck.

Hajra Delic was a nurse from Foca, a town southeast of Sarajevo. She was divorced and lived with her two sons. Since she had to support herself and her sons on one salary, money was tight.

The Yugoslavian army and the Chetniks had occupied Foca in the beginning of the war. The Yugoslavian army promised the people they would keep peace and order in the town, and most of the Muslims believed them. Hajra's older son didn't, and he escaped to Hrasnica.

Soon, a curfew was put on the town. Any Muslim found outside after 8 p.m. would be put into jail. Hajra then heard stories about Muslims killed by the Chetniks in Foca. One story was about the Chetniks killing Muslims on a bridge over the Drina River and throwing their bodies into the water.

The mass killing began in the outskirts of Foca. Only a small number were killed in Foca's center where Hajra lived. When more Muslims were killed and houses were burned near her, Hajra and her younger son decided to escape from the town. They walked through the woods. At night, they witnessed Chetniks kill other Muslims who were also trying to escape through the woods. They also saw corpses of Muslims the Chetniks had already killed and seriously wounded Muslims left in the woods to die.

Hajra and her son had left Foca at the right time. Conditions grew steadily worse there. Muslims were put into detention camps where they were beaten and tortured. The Muslims left were violently removed from their homes and forced to become refugees.

Schools, houses, and prisons throughout Foca were converted into camps where Muslim women were systematically raped and beaten. Some of those women were as young as 12 years.

The Partizan Sports Hall in Foca was used to collect Muslims to be deported. Later, it was used as a huge hall where women were continually gang raped over a period of several months. One woman reported being raped by 29 uniformed soldiers a night. Later, the hall was used as a detention center.

Many Muslims escaped to the Foca Hospital thinking they would be safe. However, the Chetniks soon entered the hospital and took it over. They took some Muslims to detention camps and executed the rest behind the hospital. Only Serbian patients would be allowed to be there.

Hajra and her son arrived in Grebak, a town in the mountains controlled by the Bosnian army. They stayed with civilians and the army. Hajra became a nurse attached to the military. When it became too dangerous to stay in Grebak, they left again and hid in the forest for six months.

"I sometimes heard shooting and knew they were killing Muslims," she said. "So we were afraid to come out. But with the winter coming, we couldn't survive in the forest for much longer, so we decided to try to escape to an area controlled by our forces."

Hajra and her son made their way to Hrasnica. She looked for and found her older son, and they moved into the upstairs flat in my building that belonged to our Serbian neighbor Tomo. I often visited Hajra and enjoyed talking to her.

Once, while I visited Hajra Delic and her youngest son in their flat, we heard a whistle and a strong explosion outside the building, and all the windows broke. A piece of shrapnel entered through a window, hit a wall, bounced off, and hit Hajra on her shoulder.

Hajra fell down and shouted, "I'm wounded! I'm wounded!"

We examined Hajra and tried to see where she was wounded. Fortunately, the shrapnel got tangled in her heavy sweater and only reddened her skin. She wasn't bleeding.

"You can stop yelling. You're not wounded and can thank your sweater," I said as I removed the hot piece of shrapnel.

A minute after, we heard shouting outside. I looked out the window, couldn't see anything, and ran outside to see my mother.

"What are you doing out here?" I asked surprised.

"It was my brother Ragab who was shouting, and he must be wounded."

We looked around and saw not her brother but Murat Medar, a neighbor. He was standing, his coat was torn, one sleeve was torn off, and if anyone had doubts he was hurt, he kept yelling, "I'm wounded!"

"Can we help you?" I asked.

"No, I"ll walk to the hospital alone," he said.

He didn't seem to be seriously wounded, so we let him go.

We were mistaken about the extent of Murat's injuries. Two days later, we heard that he died in the hospital.

We visited my uncle Ragab. He lived in a flat in another part of Hrasnica. It wasn't him who had shouted after that shell exploded, and he wasn't wounded. Ragab told us he had just received a notice to join the army. That was surprising because he had broken his leg a few years before, it never healed properly, and he had difficulties moving it.

"They can't fight a war without drafting a disabled man!" my mother shouted.

"I'm not completely disabled," Ragab said with a smile. "I'm sure the army will put me into a non-combat unit."

Ragab was proven correct. He served in a non-combat unit in the army for a year and was discharged because of his leg. He survived the war.

At the end of 1993 or the beginning of 1994, a piece of shrapnel also entered our flat. It went through a window and became embedded in the ceiling of the bedroom that Amir and I shared. Fortunately, nobody was at home during this time, except for my mother who was in another room. When I came home from the front, she told me about it. She wasn't surprised. It was just another shell explosion among many.

By this time, most of the windows in the flats around us,

including ours, were broken by the force of explosions. People put plastic sheets in their space. We did this too.

Almost every building in Hrasnica was damaged in some way. Some had shell damage or shell holes. Some were completely destroyed with their roofs gone and only some walls remaining.

The weather got colder, and since we didn't have electricity to operate the boiler, we had to use a wood burning stove for heat. Since only the people close to the stove got warm, the rest of us froze. We did a lot of shivering.

As snow began to fall, our water pumps also stopped working, so we had to wait on line at pipes and springs with containers. One time while waiting for water, I saw a French TV crew called TV#5. A man speaking French with a microphone was in front of a cameraman. They filmed the people on line and didn't speak to us. The Bosnian war was a popular international media event. Many reporters were in Sarajevo, but this was the first time I saw one. Wasn't it nice that our misery made the 6 o'clock news in Paris?

We heard that despite the shelling of civilians and the superiority in weapons of the Serbian forces over the Bosnian forces, the UN decided to keep the arms embargo on against Bosnia. I was not surprised. I once thought that the UN was here to help but now realized that most UN officials and soldiers didn't care about us and were in Bosnia just to make money.

The electricity came back again for a short time while the Serbian presidential elections were occurring in Yugoslavia, and we watched news about it on TV. The candidates were Serbian President Slobodan Milosevic and Milan Panic, a Belgrade born American citizen who had come back to Serbia recently. Milosevic would keep the war in Bosnia going, and Panic promised to end the war. Of course, we all hoped that Panic would win.

I saw Milosevic speak about the battle between the Serbs and the Muslims at Kosovo Polje in 1389, which led to the takeover of Bosnia and Serbia by the Muslim Turkish Ottoman Empire. He spoke about the many Serbian uprisings against the Muslims. Milosevic compared all Muslims and Albanians to the Turks and the Ottoman Empire. He didn't say it, but I could feel he was implying that all Muslims were bad. All in our family felt offended.

State run television stations had many programs supporting Milosevic, and government funds poured into his campaign. However, many Serbs were against his nationalistic policies, and I heard about the many demonstrations in Serbia against him, attended sometimes by people in the Orthodox hierarchy.

Milosevic was re-elected, and Panic complained that the election was fraudulent. The war in Bosnia continued.

Jasmina expected Osama to contact her after he escaped from Sarajevo. When she didn't hear from him, she assumed he wasn't able to leave the city. She was wrong. Neighbors told us that Osama finally got out of Sarajevo and was living in a small town in Bosnia with his girlfriend Edina. Jasmina was upset after hearing that.

"Before we got married, he promised to respect me, care for me, and treat me decently," she said. "Those promises meant nothing to him. I hate him."

I didn't know what to say to her.

"I'm not going to cry," she said. "I have no more tears left. I've been through all this before."

"What are you going to do?"

"After the war, I'll get a divorce and try to forget him."

"That's a good idea. You'll get over this and meet someone else."

"We'll see. I'm in no rush to get involved with another guy and get hurt again."

I hoped I would never see Osama again.

To our surprise, a day after my birthday, my father arrived at the flat.

"Are you home on a leave?" my mother asked him. "Do you have to go back?"

"No, I was discharged from the anti-terrorist force and will be with you for a long time."

Nobody asked him why he was discharged. I was comfortable with him gone and wished he would leave again.

A week later, I heard that my father's sister was killed in the town of Rogatica. The Serbs burnt her in her house, and some people said they raped her first. Earlier, his sister's son was killed in a battle for Gorazde, and her daughter was killed by a shell.

My father's sister Fatima Mehoric was a nice person, and I felt sad about her death. When tragedies occur, relatives usually comfort each other and talk about the person killed. Because of my anger with my father, I said nothing to him about it.

Chapter Six

WE JOIN THE ARMY

In February 1993, two weeks after my brother Amir's and my eighteenth birthday and 11 months after the start of the war, we received a notice to attach to the army. Amir and I were out with friends, and when we came home, my mother showed us the letter with a grave look on her face. I felt happy and excited. I had read books and seen movies about soldiers who fought in wars, and it looked like a great adventure. My mother saw the looks on our faces and didn't like it.

"You're smiling, children," she said. "You're still immature. War isn't a game. It's serious business in which people are killed."

"It's not as serious as you think it is," Amir said.

My mother kept silent. She was upset by Amir's response.

"You're not the only one who has to accept the fact that your sons have to go into the army," my father said. "It's a normal situation these days."

In the former Yugoslavia, a year of military service was compulsory for men starting in the spring or fall of their nineteenth birthday. Men between 19 and 35 could be drafted in the event of war. Exceptions were made for physical disability, and deferments were made for men entering a university. University graduates served less time. I assumed I would serve time in the military but never guessed I would be put into combat.

A day after the notice came, we went to an elementary school called Aleksasandic for medical exams. About 30 men were there, mostly our age. After waiting on line, I saw the doctor.

"Can you see and hear well?" he asked me.

"Yes."

"You have passed the medical exam and can join the army."

That was the extent of the so-called exam. Not surprisingly, Amir also passed.

A day after the exam, all of those who were called were collected in the center of Hrasnica to the place to be trained. We climbed into large trucks, and they took us through Mount Igman. It took a long time as the trucks got higher and higher. I noticed many trees cut, maybe because of shells or maybe because people cut them for firewood for heat and cooking.

We finally arrived at a large building. It was a former hotel and badly damaged. There was no roof and no windows. Plastic was on the window frames. The commander told us our training would be very intensive and last for seven days. We then went to the hotel to collect our uniforms.

We went in and waited on line. The other soldiers were our age. I recognized some from school and the neighborhood.

When I finally got to the front of the line, I was given plastic army boots. This was the entire uniform for everyone there. Army jackets, pants, and helmets were not available.

The bottom of my boots were slippery, and when I started to walk, I slid and landed on my rear. I heard laughter. Embarrassed, I stood up and carefully walked away.

We learned how to shoot and how to assemble and disassemble an automatic rifle, an AK-47. In target practice, we first used blank ammunition and then live ammunition. We had outdoor physical activities like marching, crawling, and running.

The hotel was so devastated it looked like a castle of ghosts at night. There was no heating in the rooms, and it felt as though we were sleeping outside.

In the hotel, we were gathered together and told that Hanka Paldum, a popular Bosnian folk singer, would sing for us. We applauded as Paldum got on the stage. She was in her forties and very attractive.

"I know you're nervous about going to the front line soon," she said. "I hope these songs lift your spirits. First, I'll sing a folk song."

"My days pass by.

Some other times come.

Those things that happened before.

Now they're not..." (The song sounds better in Bosnian because the words rhyme.)

Paldum's singing was beautiful, and she got tremendous applause when finished. She left the stage and shook hands with the soldiers. She said "Hello." and "How are you?" to some of them, including me.

Paldum returned to the stage and sang more folk songs, sevdalinas, and took song requests. (Sevdalinas are Bosnian love songs that existed in the days when Bosnia was part of the Ottoman Empire. Some sevdalinas are 500 years old and still popular in Bosnia. Sevdalinas are usually sad, melancholy songs about ungratified love, the longing for a better life, and the hopes that dreams will come true.)

After each song, Paldum got enthusiastic applause. Her singing was a welcome change from the misery all were experiencing.

Before the war, Paldum, a Muslim, sang and recorded songs throughout Yugoslavia. She didn't record any songs during the war. Instead, she sang regularly for Bosnian soldiers in Sarajevo and its surrounding areas. In May 1993, Paldum was one of six judges for a beauty pageant in Sarajevo, which was organized by fashion designers to raise morale. With a record playing, "Eve of Destruction," 13 young women had competed for the title of Miss Besieged Sarajevo. The winner of the contest, Imela Nogic, 17, said afterwards, "Plans? I have no plans. I may not be alive tomorrow."

In the former Yugoslavia, basic training consisted of 20 weeks of drilling, discipline, weapons assembly, weapons firing practice, tactical exercises, and political indoctrination. Because of the war, everything was speeded up. On the seventh day of training, we swore oaths to defend the country and went back to our homes to rest before being sent to the front.

The only access Sarajevo had with the rest of Bosnia was a road that went through the west of the city, through Butmir and Hrasnica. Then the road went over Mount Igman and continued to the west. (See Map Two.) On Mount Igman and other areas, much of this road was just a dirt path. Because food, supplies, and medical aid went through this road, the UN named it, "Salvation Road." We called it the "Road of Death" because it was shelled constantly, and many people traveling on it were killed. My brother and I would be sent to the third cheta (an army unit) of the 104th or night brigade, defending a section of the road on Mount Igman from being conquered by the Chetniks.

The beginning of the road went through the Butmir Airport. Because of the casualties crossing its tarmac, Bosnian miners dug a 875 yard long tunnel underneath it, which went from Dobrinja to Butmir. Work started on the tunnel in March 1993 and ended in July 1993. In the beginning, there was no electricity and no ventilation in it, so people had to use flashlights and gas masks. Later, it was permanently lit and well ventilated. The tunnel was held up by wooden stanchions, lined with planks, and was cramped and narrow. There were pumps for removing underground water, a rail track, an oil pipe, and high voltage cables, which brought electricity into Sarajevo.

Only food, medicine, army supplies, and wounded soldiers were allowed through the tunnel. Civilians had to pay to use it. The tunnel was a secret, and no reporters were allowed near it. However, it became known after more people used it, and Serbian artillery shelled its entrances. Later, when I used the tunnel, I had to wait at its entrance for hours. Soldiers were waiting before me, many of them carrying war equipment, food, and cigarettes. I heard that thousands of people passed through it daily. When I went through the tunnel, I was surprised to feel fresh air blowing through it.

Neither Amir nor I were given a rank, not even of a private. We also wouldn't receive army pay. Only cigarettes would be given out sometimes. Only at the end of the war would we receive deutschemarks. (Due to hyperinflation, the deutschemark became the official currency of Bosnia during the war, replacing the dinar.)

While waiting at home, I had a chance to think. I posed questions. How would I react when attacking an enemy position? If we were attacked by Chetniks tanks, would I hold my position or run? Would I be able to shoot another person? Would I be able to kill another person? There was a possibility of being killed, but I was more afraid of being badly wounded: either losing a limb, becoming paralyzed like my neighbor Rusid, or getting blinded. How would I react if any of those happened to me?

Amir's and my time at home was over, and we had to go to the front. We hugged our mother and sister and shook hands with our father.

A truck with other soldiers picked us up outside our apartment building and took us west on the "Road of Death" up Mount Igman. The truck turned off the main road, went on a narrow road going north, went downhill, and finally arrived at Bijela kosa, a small town near Mount Igman. Finally, we got off the truck and were directed through a forest trail to our camp. The woods were dense, and 20 minutes later, we reached a clearing and our cheta. (See Map Two.)

There was a large number of people there. Most were Muslims aged 30 to 55, and none had a uniform. If they had no rifles in their arms, nobody could say they were soldiers. They looked like a group of civilians living in their earth-covered cabins arranged like a small village that was far from the rest of the world. They looked at us but said nothing.

Looking around, we saw a woman in her early twenties with brown hair . She was short, had a round face, and was not attractive. She seemed to be the only one wearing a uniform. A medical bag with a red cross and an AK-47 were next to her. Thinking she would be the most interesting to talk to, we sat near her and introduced ourselves. She said her name was Safi. She was the only woman in this group. I looked at her medical bag.

"Are you a nurse or soldier?" I asked.

"Both. Before the war, I went to nursing school, and I give first aid to wounded people. I was also in the commandos and was trained to use artillery and mortars."

I had heard that many women became soldiers in our army and was about to ask Safi about the commandos, but she changed the subject.

"You are young," she said to us. "How old are you?"

"We are eighteen," I answered.

"Both? You're twins?"

"Yes."

"Believe it or not, this is the first time I have met twins."

"Really."

"Who is older?"

"I am older," my brother said.

"I have heard that twins are very close and devoted to each other. Is this the case with you?"

"Yes, we love each other very much," I said.

My mind flashed back to an earlier time. As he left childhood, Amir's personality changed. Because he was two hours and 15 minutes older than I, he decided he was a more important person who should be respected more. He also got angry easily. Perhaps his aggressiveness had to do with his physical changes. He grew slightly taller than I and was wide-shouldered. (I grew to be six feet.) I understood that Amir's new attitude wasn't against me. He was trying to establish a personality. Even through Amir and I had many quarrels (a quarrel or two each month), I realized that we loved each other very much and would die for each other.

"Do you believe in telepathy?" Safi asked us.

"What a curious girl," I thought. How did questions about my brother and me turn into a discussion of telepathy?

Safi explained she had heard that people who are very close to each other such as twins are sometimes known for knowing each other's thoughts and feelings even when they're far apart. She wondered if we ever had similar experiences. We told Safi that from our mannerisms, we could sometimes tell what each other was thinking about, but that wasn't telepathy.

Our discussion was interrupted when a man in his forties wearing a uniform walked up to us.

"Welcome novices," he said. "My nickname is Izo, and I'm your commander." Amir and I stood up and introduced ourselves.

"Who would like to be with the novices?" Izo asked the

other soldiers sitting around. I felt embarrassed when I saw all the people just staring at us with their eyes wide open as if we had just fallen from space. Izo waited patiently, but nobody said anything. It was obvious nobody wanted to be with us.

"Merhaba!" came from somewhere, interrupting the silence. "Merhaba" is a Turkish greeting that means, "Hello." This greeting is used only by Muslims in Bosnia. We turned to see the speaker of the greeting, a strong, wide-shouldered, attractive man of medium height aged about 35, wearing civilian clothes with fair hair and blue eyes.

"My name is Ferid Mozderac," the man introduced himself to me.

"My name is Elvir Kulin. It's nice to meet you. This is my brother Amir."

"Hello," Amir said.

"Ferid, it seems to me that nobody wants to be with the novices," Izo said. "So, I want you to take them with you to the front line if you don't mind."

"What a nice welcome!" Ferid said looking at the soldiers with his eyes blazing with anger before he took us to his place. He handed me an AK-47 and carried one himself. There was no gun available for my brother.

After 15 minutes of walking through the woods, we reached an earth-covered cabin camouflaged by many branches and leaves. Ferid took us into the cabin, and we saw ammunition and four hand grenades.

"Guys, this is our home," Ferid said. "How do you like it?"

"It's very nice," I said with a forced smile. Ferid knew I was lying.

There was a small trench in front of the cabin, and we jumped into it. We looked over the top. I saw cabins and trenches to the right and left of us. In front of us were many trees so thick we couldn't see 110 yards past them.

Around 55 yards to the left and right of us were our other cabins and trenches. Opposite us were the Chetnik trenches, which we couldn't see because of the trees. Behind the Chetnik trenches were the towns of Vrelo Bosne and Vrutci. Above and behind us were Bijela kosa and the "Road of Death" on Mount Igman. Between us and the Chetnik trenches were land mines.

"Don't walk on the field in front of us without orders, or you might step on a mine and be killed or wounded," Ferid said. "You have to be on guard. The Chetniks are close. The 'Road of Death' is the only communication between Sarajevo and the rest of the world. If we aren't careful, the Chetniks might conquer part of the 'Road of Death,' and all of Sarajevo would be in danger."

Rifle shots in the distance punctuated his statements, and as we spoke, we heard more rifle shots and automatic fire bursts, mostly from the Chetnik side.

"The Chetniks have a huge amount of ammunition and don't hesitate to use it," Ferid said. "We're short of ammunition, so only use it when you have to. We only have two automatics, so we'll take turns holding them. For two hours, you two will stay in the trench armed, and I'll relax in the cabin. For the next two hours, I'll stay in the trench armed, and you two will relax in the cabin."

I guessed that Ferid felt brave enough to keep guard alone, but I was becoming afraid with the periodic gunfire.

"There are four grenades in the cabin," Ferid said. "Only use them if the enemy is right in front of you. If you use a grenade and no enemy was there, you could go to prison. There aren't enough grenades, and we can't waste them." Later, Izo also warned us about using the grenades.

Ferid told us that every two days, we were relieved from the trench and went back to those earth-covered cabins behind us to relax and eat. After two days, we came back to the trench again. After a few months, we could go back to our homes to shower and change our clothes. When we went back to our homes and how long we stayed there depended on how severe the fighting was.

"At night, you'll hear rumbling from the Chetnik side," Ferid said. "Those are their tanks, but don't worry. This forest is unsuitable for tanks to go through."

The Ardennes Forest in Belgium was said to be unsuitable for tanks to go through, but the German army had gone through it twice during World War II. Hopefully, the Chetniks didn't learn strategy from the Germans. I wouldn't like to see a tank coming at us.

Ferid warned us about lighting a fire in the trench because the Chetniks aimed their artillery at that light. Later, three Bosnian soldiers didn't pay attention to that warning, and a shell hit their position. Two of those soldiers were killed, and the third was wounded.

The three of us spent most of that day together in the trench laughing at the jokes we told each other. Most of them were vulgar but good. Ferid would occasionally interrupt the conversation to yell something across to the Chetniks, but he got no response. After laughing at a funny joke, we heard something from the Chetnik side.

"Hey, stop laughing!" someone yelled. "You're so boring!"

"Okay, we'll stop laughing, but only if you can do me a favor!" Ferid yelled back.

"What favor?!" the Chetnik asked.

"Well, I have a problem with my dick! It's so hard! Could you send your mother here to soften it for me?!"

"Well, I'll see what I can do about that! Wait a minute please!" the Chetnik yelled back politely.

After a minute, automatic gunfire hit the ground and trees in front of us, and we quickly crouched lower into the trench.

We heard whistling and explosions as shells landed near us, and dirt fell into the trench. It seemed to me we couldn't survive for long with those outbursts of fire. After 15 minutes, the firing stopped.

"I don't like that answer to my question at all," Ferid said. Then he laughed. "I'm going into the cabin now to get my two hours of rest."

I looked at Ferid leaving and looked at my brother.

"What do you think of him?" I asked.

Amir kept silent for a while and finally said, "I think he's crazy and might get us killed."

It got dark. I had never been alone in the woods at night. It was a strange experience. I heard some animals moving around and the distant rumbling of Chetnik tanks. They made the only noise because the gunfire had stopped.

We heard something moving in front of us for a while, then it stopped, and we heard breathing. Then it moved again for a while, then stopped again, and again we heard breathing. Who could that be? I didn't see anything in the woods. Amir and I looked at each other. I'd never been so frightened. The noise sounded like a man. Perhaps the Chetnik that Ferid insulted was coming to kill us. The sound terrified us.

The next time it moved, Amir shot in its direction. It stopped, and we heard breathing again. Ferid got out of the cabin, and we explained what we heard.

"That's not a Chetnik. That's a porcupine," Ferid explained. "They sound just like a man. Don't waste your bullets shooting at it." He went back into the cabin.

Amir and I spent our first night on the front line listening to animals, moving tanks, and distant gunfire. Soldiers' experiences in war movies looked much more interesting and heroic. I had never seen a movie that showed troops able to shout at each other from their trenches. And I'd never seen one with a soldier who walked or rode home periodically to shower and change clothes. And the lack of ammunition, guns, and uniforms seemed all wrong. It was not the way movies depicted war. Of course, I'd never known what war would be like when it came close to home. I wished I had never had to learn it either.

In the morning, we heard sporadic shooting, shelling, laughing, talking, and singing from both sides of the front. (Shooting and shell explosions were regular sounds in Bijela kosa. The Chetniks used different calibers of artillery against us, including 82 mm, 122 mm, 155 mm, and anti-aircraft shells.) The Chetnik voices were far away, and I couldn't understand what they were saying. Were any of them my former Serbian friends or neighbors?

There was shooting from our side for a long time and our commander's voice yelling, "We don't have enough ammunition! Save it for when the enemy attacks!"

We didn't hear any praying from our side, which didn't surprise me. Bosnian Muslims require a clean place to pray in public, and a dirty trench isn't suitable. According to Islam, the mandatory prayers of worship (called the Salat) should be performed only after a Muslim's body and clothes are cleaned of all dirt. But we often quietly prayed to God in private, particularly when we were being shelled.

A few birds landed near us, chirped, and flew off. Were they welcoming us to the neighborhood or laughing at our situation? We didn't know, but their songs were pleasant and made us smile. Singing birds became our regular visitors for most days.

"Good morning," Ferid said when he joined us in the trench.

"Good morning," Amir and I responded.

"Are you going to provoke the Chetniks on a regular basis?" Amir asked him.

Ferid laughed. "I don't have a mortar to attack the Chetniks, so I attack them with insults. Also, it uses up their ammunition."

We told each other about ourselves. Ferid said he was married, didn't have children, and had mostly worked as a construction worker before the war.

Ferid spoke about his wife. He missed her companionship and was worried about her living in a city under siege.

In response to questions, Ferid said his wife wasn't able to conceive. "My wife and I tried very hard to have a baby but couldn't. She's very upset about it. We went to the doctor, she took fertility drugs, but still no child."

I suggested to Ferid that he and his wife might think about adopting a child.

"I've no problem with adopting. I spoke to my wife about that, but she wants to give birth to her own child first." He smiled. "I'm not worried about it. When my wife is ready, we'll adopt."

Ferid told us about his other job as a truck driver. He drove a truck all over Yugoslavia and admitted while on the road, he chased after women and had sex with many of them. He said his secret of getting so many women to have sex with him was that he bought them gifts. He also admitted he kept having sex with women after he got married.

"Being on the road for long periods of time got lonely," he explained.

Ferid said his wife didn't know about the women, and if she found out, she would divorce him.

I disapproved of Ferid's conduct but said nothing.

Ferid smiled. "I remember one particular girl I met," he said. "Some people in Yugoslavia are poor, and because some women can't afford cars, they have to hitchhike. I saw a young, attractive woman hitchhiking and picked her up. We spoke, I took her out to eat, and I bought her gifts. On the road, I stopped the truck, we looked at each other, and I knew she was mine. We hugged and kissed, and I drove to a motel. In the room, we kissed some more. She removed her clothes, and I removed mine..." In graphic detail, Ferid described what that woman's body looked like, where he touched her, and what they did sexually.

After that, Ferid's sexual experiences on the road became the main topic of his conversation. In detail, he described how he met the woman, how her body parts looked, and the sexual acts they performed. After a while, each story sounded the same, and I became bored hearing them.

We finally went to the earth-covered cabins, ate, relaxed, and met the soldiers from our cheta and our brigade. Most were Muslims. One was a Serbian. Several were Croatians. One of Croats was named Dusko, (he was my neighbor) another was named Jozo, and another, Denis, was a child from a mixed marriage. His mother was a Muslim, and his father was a Croatian. (There were many children of mixed marriages in Bosnia.) The army food consisted of beans, some kind of stew with fats in it, and water. While Amir looked for better food, I walked around, met Safi again, and she told me more about her life.

Safi was born in Kukurevici, a small village in Serbia near the Bosnian border. Mostly Muslims lived there, and it was "ethnically cleansed" and completely destroyed in 1992 when the war broke out in Bosnia. Safi and her family were forced to leave, and they became separated in their flight. Safi went to Bosnia, joined the Bosnian army, and took part in several battles as a soldier and nurse.

I asked Safi about her family. She said for a long time, she didn't know whether they were alive or not. Fortunately with the help of the Red Cross, she contacted them. They were living in Turkey.

"I live for the day when I'll see them again," she said. Tears came, and she cried.

Amir and I went back and forth between the front and the earth-covered cabins. One time, at the cabins, we were surprised to see Musec Kenad, who had been in primary school with us. Musec seemed glad to see us even though in school we had hardly spoken to one another.

The main topic of discussion at the cabins was Safi. Male soldiers were friendly when talking to her. However, behind her back, many of them (single and married) bragged about how they would get her to have sex with them. Also, I noticed that many of the soldiers cursed constantly.

One of those soldiers got together with Safi but not the way he wanted. He was cutting wood with an small ax nearby. I heard a yell, went to the sound, and saw that he had cut off a finger. Only a piece of skin was attached to his hand. Safi bandaged the wound, and he was sent to the hospital.

Ferid also bragged he would get Safi to go to bed with him and constantly described in graphic detail what he would do with her sexually.

As far as we knew, none of the soldiers succeeded in their quest. Safi was friendly with them, but it ended there.

The Serb in our brigade ran away to the Chetnik trenches. Soon after he left, there was a lot of shelling and gunfire which came close to our positions in the trenches and the earth-covered cabins. He probably gave our positions to the Serbian artillery because he knew them. Because of that, many soldiers in my brigade didn't trust Serbian soldiers serving with us.

Another time, when I returned to the earth-covered cabins, I talked with Safi again. She was brave, sociable, and liked to tell jokes. While talking, we heard someone calling for help. Safi picked up her first aid bag and said, "Let's go."

We went to the sound of the voice and saw a middle aged

soldier going through the woods. He wasn't walking properly, so we knew something was wrong with his leg. We didn't expect him to be wounded seriously because he was able to stay on his feet, but we were wrong.

"Lie down, please," Safi said to the man. "Elvir, come and help me."

We tried to take his pants off but in vain. Each time we tried, he yelled in agony. So we tore the leg of his pants. Quite a big piece of his muscle was missing, and he was bleeding badly.

"Let me see my leg!" the man shouted as he tried to sit up. He was very frightened.

"I'm afraid I will not let you see it because I don't want you to panic without reason," Safi said calmly with a smile. "Believe it or not, it's only a scratch."

That remark made the man calm and ready to cooperate with us. Safi bandaged his leg.

I got a stretcher, and we brought the man to a cabin. As an ambulance took him away, Safi said he would never be able to walk properly.

"How could you pretend that everything was okay?"

"Elvir, my job is to help people, not to tell them the truth," she said and walked away.

I had never thought about nurses and doctors not telling the absolute truth to patients. But how would the truth have helped this frightened, wounded man at that moment? I understood that honesty was sometimes not the best way.

There was another woman soldier in Bijela kosa. Her name was Havka. She was shy, intelligent, and pretty. Soldiers relied on her; she didn't run away from the front. Havka was from a town in eastern Bosnia. When the Yugoslavian army occupied that town, she was forced to leave and became a refugee. She went to Grebak where she saw many dead people who were killed by the Chetniks. Havka then went from army unit to army unit. When I asked her about her house, family, and childhood, she became nervous and started to cry. So I changed the subject. As with Safi, male soldiers bragged about how they would get Havka to have sex with them. But as far as I knew, Havka wasn't interested in that.

Whenever a shell landed in Hrasnica or Sarajevo and many civilians were killed, the soldiers were upset because a family member might be one of the casualties. Because of that, they were happier when the front line was shelled heavily instead of urban areas.

The front line at Bijela kosa was shelled constantly, but I knew of no cases of "shell shock" or "combat fatigue." Only one soldier I knew went crazy during the war. Because of an argument with his wife, he threw his child out of the third floor window of his flat, killing him. When the police arrived at his flat to arrest him, he threw himself out of the same window, killing himself.

I enjoyed Amir's company in the trench because he always had amusing stories to tell. One sunny day in May, in the middle of one of his stories, artillery fire came from the Serbian side and this time, the whistling and explosions kept getting closer. After an hour, they stopped. We thought they would continue the shooting, but they didn't.

"For God's sake, what's going on with this?" Amir asked. "Are they trying to target us?" He was as frightened as I was.

"Who knows?" I answered quietly in order to hide my fear and calm him down.

It was as quiet as if everything had disappeared from the face of the earth. We even noticed the absence of the birds' singing that we enjoyed listening to.

"Would you like to hear a really good joke, Elvir?" Amir asked.

"It amazes me that anyone could ask such a stupid question," I said smiling at him. "You know I've always loved jokes."

As Amir was telling his joke, artillery fire started again, and the explosions were again near us. Then they stopped. Amir finished telling his joke, and as he began to tell another one, we heard something like a twig snapping. Amir kept quiet.

"What's that?" he finally said.

I listened but didn't hear anything more. "Don't pay attention. It's probably an animal."

Amir continued to tell jokes but stopped when he heard voices. We weren't sure if they were human voices. We became silent and heard twigs breaking again. As time passed, the voices became louder. Two men appeared in front of us, walking through the woods as if they were walking to a picnic. They were calm and moved slowly. We kept silent, and I felt frightened. They had beards, uniforms, rifles, and white armbands. One had dark hair, and the other had reddish hair. There was no doubt they were Serbian soldiers. We loaded and aimed our automatics and waited for them to get nearer so we would have a larger target.

We fired a burst at their chest area, saw leaves flying off the tree branches near them, and saw smoke in front of our guns. The Chetniks disappeared, and we didn't hear voices. Soon, Izo came to our trench, and behind him was Ferid who had been resting in the cabin.

"What happened?" Izo asked.

"We saw Serbian soldiers and fired at them," I said.

Izo smiled at us. "Are you sure you saw Serbian soldiers? Calm down, and shoot only when you have to. There's not enough ammunition." Then he left. Izo didn't believe us because we were novices. He made us wonder if we had shot Serbian soldiers or not.

The next day, near the spot where the uniformed people

were seen, our soldiers found a rucksack with blood spots on it.

I answered a question I had asked myself before I came to the front line: Would I be able to shoot another person? The answer was yes. I didn't feel any physical or emotional distress shooting at and wounding those Chetniks. They were armed and approaching our position. They would have shot at Amir and me if we hadn't shot at them. It was two less Chetniks to terrorize Muslims, at least for the time they were in the hospital.

In our brigade, we had people called moles because they did what moles did; they dug trenches. Mostly, they were mobilized older disabled soldiers, but some were Bosnian Serbs who refused to join the Chetniks but also refused to join the Bosnian army.

While at the earth-covered cabins, Izo gave me an assignment about the Serbian moles. "A group of them will be escorted here soon. Your job is to distribute shovels, take them to the front line, and have them dig trenches. If they try to escape to the Serbian side, shoot them." He gave me a map of where they were to dig.

I didn't like the assignment and was sure I wouldn't shoot at them if they tried to escape. I hoped none of them would make the attempt.

10 men escorted by a Bosnian soldier arrived. I handed shovels to them. They didn't speak. All were around my age except a man who was in his fifties. I recognized him. His name was Krsto, and he was my former elementary school teacher. He taught shop: electricity, metal working, wood working, and drafting.

As Krsto looked at me now, I felt embarrassed and ashamed.

I wanted to say something to him but didn't know what. So I offered him a cigarette.

"Let's go," I said leading the way. The other soldier took the rear. The Serbs looked afraid of going to the front.

When we got to the front line, I ordered them to dig, which they did. Finally, the trenches were dug, and we escorted them back.

Amir and I went back and forth between Hrasnica (home) and Bijela kosa (the front) many times. It was suggested we walk there and back because the Chetniks shelled trucks traveling in that area. Because the journey took two and a half hours to walk, with part of it climbing up and down Mount Igman, Amir and I preferred to hitch rides on trucks. The trucks usually rode there at night or early in the morning with their lights off. Sometimes, we were in a truck when it was shelled. When that happened, the driver rode faster. He never stopped because the road was narrow, and there was no place to pull off to the side and hide. A stationary truck in the middle of the road was an easy target for the Serbian artillery.

Sometimes, when Amir and I walked to and from Bijela kosa, we went near an artillery spotter position our forces had on Mount Igman. There were fewer trees there than at the front, and when we looked down toward the front lines, we could see our own and the Chetnik trenches. We also saw Serbian T-55 tanks moving around. They constantly moved to prevent them from being targeted and shelled.

One time, when we returned to Hrasnica, we saw a small shell hole on the outside wall of our building at the second floor level. I asked about the hole and was told that the Serbs had shelled us heavily a few months after we last left for the front. That mortar hit Hajra Delic's flat. Fortunately, nobody was hurt. Two other mortars hit the roof and caused damage. Water came now into the upper flats when it rained.

I visited Delic and asked about that shell. "It was terrible," she said. "My sons and I were eating in the dining room. I heard an explosion, some of the wall came in, and thick fog went through the flat. It was very confusing."

Delic also told me that the Bosnian army mobilized her two sons.

"What about you?" I asked. "Are you going to work as a nurse at a hospital here?"

"I spoke about that with my sons. They said with them in the army, they didn't want me in the army too. It would be too dangerous. I agreed to their requests."

Hospitals in Hrasnica were regularly shelled by the Chetniks.

**MAP ONE – BOSNIA AND THE OTHER YUGOSLAVIAN
REPUBLICS OF SERBIA, SLOVENIA, CROATIA, AND
MACEDONIA**

MAP TWO – SARAJEVO

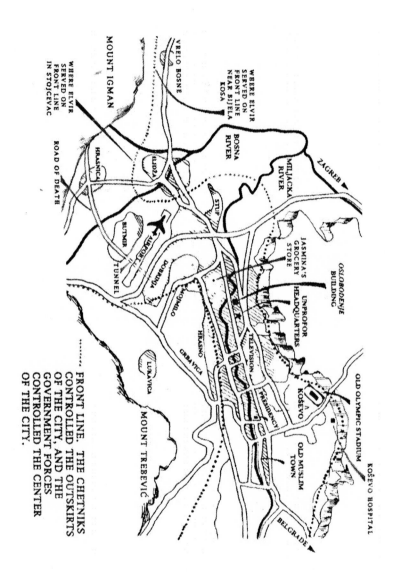

PHOTOGRAPHS

Inside Jasmina's grocery store, "Osama" at the end of 1991.
From left: Fadila, Safet, and Elvir Kulin.

Bosnian soldiers near the front line outside Sarajevo in July 1995.
From left: Ershef Kulin and Safet Ajanovic.
(Safet Ajanovic served with Ershef Kulin in the anti-terrorist force and
the commandos. Elvir Kulin met Safet two or three times but didn't
know him very well.)

Elvir Kulin in front of a kindergarten destroyed by a Serbian shell in central Sarajevo, January 2001.

In a flat in central Sarajevo. From left: Elvir Kulin and Maury Hirschkorn, January 2001.

In Elvir's flat in Hrasnica. From left: Jasmina Gradulo, Ziza Kulin, Elvir Kulin, and Ershef Kulin, January 2001.

In Elvir's flat in Hrasnica. From left: Amir Kulin and Elvir Kulin, January 2001.

Elvir Kulin in front of a grocery store/restaurant in central Sarajevo, January 2001.

Jasmina Gradulo, 1999.

Elvir's apartment building in Hrasnica. Notice the mortar shell hole on the wall of the building, January 2001.

The flat across Elvir's courtyard that was destroyed by a Serbian katyusha, January 2001.

The ruins of the Oslobodjenje building, which housed the only Sarajevian newspaper to function during the war, January 2001.

The ruins of Sarajevo's main nursing home, January 2001.

In a Bosnian Trench

The bottom part of a trench in Stojcevac, December, 2001.

A ruined house behind the Bosnian trench in Stojcevac, December 2001.

The former front line in Stojcevac.
The tape marks where the minefield is, December 2001.

The former front line in Stojcevac, December 2001.

ELVIR KULIN'S ARMY IDENTIFICATION CARD

Notice the word "Ilidza" on the identification card. Ilidza stands for the Sarajevian district of Ilidza where Hrasnica is located, not the settlement of Ilidza.

ELVIR KULIN'S ARMY ENLISTMENT DOCUMENT

REPUBLIKA BOSNA I HERCEGOVINA

SVEČANA OBAVEZA

JA _____ **KULIN ELVIR**

ZAKLINJEM SE DA ĆU BRANITI NEZAVISNOST SUVERENOST I CJELOVITOST REPUBLIKE BOSNE I HERCEGOVINE, DA ĆU SAVJESNO I DISCIPLINOVANO IZVRŠAVATI SVE OBAVEZE I DUŽNOSTI PRIPADNIKA ARMIJE REPUBLIKE BOSNE I HERCEGOVINE, DA ĆU BRANITI NJENU SLOBODU I ČAST I U TOJ BORBI ISTRAJATI.

ILIDŽA, **09 03 '93**   KOMANDANT

ELVIR KULIN'S ARMY DISCHARGE PAPER

ODLUKBNA KI. UBLIKE
VOJhA .AJ6A
FOVJIKIJIVO

Ne osnovu člana 97. Zakona o službi u A R BiH ("Sl.list R BiH br.
11/92, 8. '3, 17/93, 1/94, 16/94, 4/95 i 2o/95), a u vezi sa članom
2o2. Zako.a : rpštem upravnom postupku, rješavajući o otpustu iz Armije
R BiH v/c ___ _KuLiN_(_fRSEF)_EČViR._____ donosim,

R J L I L NJ E

1. Otpušt; se iz A R LiH v/o __ _KUG·N_ _ELViRJ___ ,pripadnik
   VJ 5o(3.

2. Imenovani se otpušta iz A R BiH dana _24.04._ 199£ god. kada mu
   prests ;e svojstvo vojnog lica.

3. Po pravosnažncsti rjošenja, imetovani se briše iz evidencije
   pripadnika VJ 5o63, zaključuje mu se vojnička knjižica i isti se
   razdnžuje sa naoružanjem i opremom.

4. Nadležno OnO u opčini _/Li m7_ će imenovanom regulisati daljnji RR.

O B R A Z L C . E NJ E

g··· /7 r3. ..1996 god. ovoj komandi dostavljeno je naredjenje komande VJ
5o31_ 06/2-1-6_ _ _ _ da se izvrši otpust iz A R LiH po osnovu
provodjenja Dejtonskog sporazuma o smanjivanju aktivnog sastava OL R BiH.

U postupku za otpust utvrdjeno je da imenovani ne ispunjava uslove za
aktivni sast:y A R BiH a,ioti se nije ni prijavi ze aktivnu službu, pa
je doneseno rješenje kao u dispozitivu istpg.

Protiv ovog rješenja može :e izjaviti žalba u roku od 8 dana od dana
prijema rješenja. Je'ba ·· is ;.vl··'e komandantu VJ 5o31, a predaje
se putem ove komanu..

F/AG

Radjeno u 4 primjerka i
ostavlgeno:
imenovano
Orgar 73 i H
ONO
s/s

KOMANDANT
major
lizović

ELVIR KULIN'S ARMY CERTIFICATE THAT WAS PROMISED TO BE EXCHANGED FOR MONEY

REPUBLIKA BOSNA I HERCEGOVINA
FEDERACIJA BOSNE I HERCEGOVINE
MINISTARSTVO ODBRANE - OBRANE

Ev.bz. 493092906689
Odjeljenje u općini ILIDŽA
Datum: 26.08.1996.

UVJERENJE

o plaćama
pripadnika Oružanih snaga
Republike Bosne i Hercegovine

1. Prezime	KULIN
2. Ime oca	KASIM
3. Ime	ELVIR
4. JMB	0602975171507
5. Broj vojne knjižice	2289887
6. U vojnoj evidenciji	ILIDŽA 29
7. Status pripadnika OS	14
8. Vrijeme provedeno u OS	od 01.03.93. do 22.04.96.

	od	do
	dan mj. god.	dan mj. god.

9. Broj mjeseci za plaću	38
10. Mjesečni iznos plaće u DEM	400
11. Ukupni iznos plaće u DEM	15200
12. Isplaćeno ranije u DEM	/
13. Ukupno za isplatu u DEM	15200

Ukupno za isplatu u DEM (slovima) /petnaesthiljadadvijestotine/

SAGLASAN: SNAGE R BIH   MINISTARSTVO ODBRANE - OBRANE
Elvir
(pripadnik OS – potpis)   (M.P. i potpis)   (M.P. i potpis)

CHAPTER SEVEN

WE RECAPTURE MOUNT IGMAN

At the beginning of August 1993, using tanks, artillery, and troops, the Serbs took Mount Bjelasnica, Mount Igman, and part of the "Road of Death" that ran through Mount Igman. Mount Bjelasnica is located south of Mount Igman. Mount Igman was the only high ground around Sarajevo that wasn't occupied by the Serbs.

With the capture of Mount Igman, Sarajevo was completely surrounded. It also meant the city of Gorazde would also suffer. When the Chetniks cut the roads to Gorazde, the only way to get food and supplies to it was to bring them over Mount Igman. With the capture of that mountain, people in Gorazde would starve.

Threatened by NATO air strikes against their new positions, General Mladic announced that his troops would withdraw from those heights. However as the days passed, Serbian troops were reinforced not withdrawn.

I was at home when this happened and heard the news from an army messenger. Since this was the responsibility of my brigade, my brother and I would have to leave immediately for the front.

My mother looked worried. "Be careful boys. Promise you'll stick together and protect each other."

We promised.

A truck brought us to a spot in the woods, and we walked through it in small groups in order not to be seen. We arrived in a clearing and waited while more soldiers from our brigade joined us. I saw Ferid, Safi, Musec Kenad, and other soldiers I recognized. Izo arrived and was joined by another uniformed officer in his late thirties who spoke to us.

"My name is Jepa, and I'll be your commander for this operation. The Chetniks took part of the 'Road of Death.' Guys, we're going to attack them tomorrow before they fortify. We can't let them control that road or the people in Sarajevo will starve. We must take it back at all cost, no matter how many soldiers die, and with Allah's help, we will succeed."

While we waited, soldiers spoke to each other. We knew our army was in a bad situation. The Chetniks had superior and more numerous weapons, and many of us would be killed.

"If someone deserts during the battle, we should agree to shoot him in the back," Ferid said.

"Is that necessary?" I asked.

"Yes, people will be afraid to desert because of that. Are we agreed?"

We all agreed, but I hoped I wouldn't be put in that situation.

There weren't enough rifles for everybody, so soldiers without ones would stay behind to support us with food, water, ammunition, and relieve us when we got tired. Amir, Ferid, Safi, Musec Kenad, and I were given rifles.

Army jackets arrived, but there was a small number of them. There were 12 soldiers in an odjeljemje (a small unit), and four odjeljemje in a cheta. We got only one army jacket for our odjeljemje and decided to put 12 pieces of paper into a hat.

One piece was marked, and the soldier who picked the marked paper would get the jacket. My brother Amir got the marked paper and thus the jacket.

The next day we were ready to attack.

"Remember our promise to our mother," I said to Amir. "We'll stick together."

Ferid and some other soldiers approached us.

"Boys, please keep separated," Ferid said. "I wouldn't like you both to be killed."

"But Ferid, who would keep my brother's back better than I?" I asked.

"I know what you're saying, but your mother..."

"We'll keep together whether you like it or not!" Amir interrupted him.

Ferid and the other soldiers walked away.

Jepa called us together. "It's time, guys. I'll lead you through the woods to the Chetnik positions. Keep as quiet as you can, and no talking. Good luck."

We marched up Mount Igman through the forest. Amir walked next to me. Not a sound was heard except for our feet hitting twigs and fallen leaves. Jepa was holding a walkie-talkie. We reached the top of the mountain and continued to walk. We were aware we were in a vulnerable position, and if the Chetniks ambushed us, most of us would be killed or wounded without accomplishing our mission. But we didn't hear a sound from them. With hand movements, Jepa ordered us to crawl and keep as quiet as possible. We approached a clearing, and the soldiers in front stopped. Jepa had us spread out, and we approached the Chetniks so close we could see them among the trees in front of us. Some were digging a trench, while others were keeping guard with rifles. All were wearing uniforms. Amir and other soldiers stuck branches into their jackets for camouflage, but I didn't. We watched the Chetniks for some time waiting for the order to start firing. Most of us were nervous and frightened. On the ground behind some trees, I saw the faces of soldiers, and they were covered in sweat.

I heard the commander say, "It's time to attack." I heard someone yell, "Allahu Ekber!" which in Arabic is, "Allah is the greatest!" and we all ran out of the woods toward the Chetniks yelling, "Allahu Ekber!" while shooting at them.

The Chetniks looked at us with surprised, confused expressions, ducked into their trench, and shot in our direction. I saw some Chetniks shoot in different directions proving they weren't sure where we were. I shot my rifle at them. Fire from their trench stopped, but we still ran toward it, yelling and shooting. As I got closer, I was preparing to face them in hand-to-hand combat. I jumped into their trench and was surprised to see nothing. There were no Chetniks, not even a dead or wounded one. We must have been terrible marksmen. I saw Amir behind me.

I thought the fight was over but saw our soldiers jump out of the Chetnik trench and chase after them downhill. The Chetniks were retreating. Amir and I ran after them. We heard more shooting. After running for about 30 minutes, we heard whistles and saw explosions of Serbian shells around us. I was most afraid of a shell exploding in a tree near us (called a tree burst) because its shrapnel would cover a larger area than a shell exploding on the ground (called a ground burst). Each time we heard a whistle close by, we hit the ground as the shell exploded near us. I saw that Amir ran ahead of me, and I chased after him.

To my right, I saw Safi running and shouting, "Allahu Ekber!" A shell exploded near her, and the detonation was so strong that she flew over my head, did a somersault and fell to earth. I examined her and saw no injuries.

"Are you wounded?" I asked.

Safi shook her head no but couldn't talk. She had fallen so hard that she was gasping for breaths; her chest was heaving up and down. I wanted to stay until she recovered but was separated from my brother and had to catch up with him and the rest of the brigade.

"I have to join the brigade to push back the Chetniks," I said. "If I don't see you, I'll send a first aid man to this spot." She nodded.

I left her and ran through the woods down the mountain. I kept hearing explosions and saw smoke from explosions around me. Finally, I caught up with Amir and told him about Safi.

About two hours after we attacked the Serb trench, we reached the outskirts of the town of Siljak. The Chetniks had occupied this town, and now we did. Jepa was there and ordered us to dig a trench. We couldn't do it because we didn't have shovels and the ground was rock hard. So we piled stones in front of us. Shells fell around us, and each time we heard a whistle, we hit the ground.

Safi arrived later and also piled stones. She said she felt better. I was glad she wasn't touched by shrapnel. I heard about other people who were blown into the air by shell explosions, but they were killed or badly wounded.

We heard more whistles near us, and everyone around me hugged the ground. I got down behind my stones and tried to make myself as small as possible. There were violent explosions nearby, and small stones and dirt fell around us. I lifted my head up and saw nobody around me was hurt. We continued to pile stones.

I felt a few drops of water hit my shoulder, and then there was a downpour. With us out in the open, this was no time for rain. I hoped it would stop, but it just kept coming, soaking all of us. We didn't have raincoats or anything to cover ourselves.

My clothes, skin, and hair got soaked. I noticed that the Chetnik shelling had stopped.

It continued to rain heavily for hours, and no protection reached us. We were ordered to hold our positions and wait. Fortunately, the Chetniks didn't counterattack, and we didn't see or hear their tanks. But we were wet, tired, cold, and felt miserable.

Finally the rain stopped, the sun found us, and our clothes dried out. We heard that four or five soldiers from my cheta were killed during the battle, and a greater number were wounded, including Musec Kenad who received a bad foot wound.

From our position, we saw Siljak behind us. It was a town of mostly small houses, local people going to the fields, and cows and sheep milling about. Our troops had to fight to capture Siljak, and a soldier I knew, Edriz, was killed in that battle.

12 days after, when Siljak was fortified, Amir and I went home to finish our leave.

Our troops were successful in almost every battle they had fought recently, and the "Road of Death" was cleared. However, Serbian troops still controlled a smaller part of Mount Bjelasnica and a smaller part of Mount Igman. Given an ultimatum that there would be NATO air strikes by a certain date, they finally withdrew from those areas and were replaced immediately by about 300 French UN troops. Soon, UN troops took control of all of Mount Igman.

After our leave was over, Amir and I went to another area near Siljak. It was similar to Bijela kosa in that the front line consisted of camouflaged cabins and trenches at the front, earth-covered cabins behind the line and a minefield between our and the Chetnik positions. There were sparser woods there than near Bijela kosa, but when we looked toward the Chetnik lines, we just saw trees. Because our army leaders were afraid that the Chetniks would counterattack and try to recapture Siljak, we stayed and didn't return to Bijela kosa. Jepa was our commander. Their fears were unfounded. Siljak was under our control for the rest of the war.

Amir and I kept guard alone at one of the trenches and cabins. I rested for a few hours in the cabin while he was in the trench and vice versa. After a few days, we were relieved and rested at the earth-covered cabins. There, we met other soldiers we knew including Ferid and Safi, who were guarding other sections around Siljak.

Even though the Chetniks never attacked, they sent artillery and automatic fire in our direction and around us. The shells were mostly the same caliber as they used in Bijela kosa. Sometimes the shooting would go on for hours.

We heard that a soldier I sometimes kept guard with, Vaha, was killed. Chetniks quietly approached his position, and when he looked up, they sprayed machine gun fire at him. The bullets hit him in the head.

While resting at the cabins, Jepa gave me an assignment about Vaha. "Vaha was taken off the front line into the forest. Other soldiers are guarding his body in shifts to keep the animals away. I want you to be the next shift and guard him until a truck takes him away." He told me where Vaha was lying.

I walked through the woods and relieved the guard who was guarding Vaha's body. Vaha's face and body were covered with nettles to keep insects away. His feet were sticking out.

I knew Vaha by sight and sometimes had talked to him. He was a refugee from Foca and had told me that some of his family members were killed by the Chetniks when they occupied that town. He was with my cheta in Bijela kosa and when we attacked the "Road of Death." Vaha was 32 and of average height.

I couldn't resist a look at Vaha and removed the nettles.

The left side of his face was torn away by bullets. I felt sick and quickly put back the nettles.

After a few hours, two people came with a stretcher and took Vaha away.

Finally, Amir and I went back to our homes and discovered that the food situation had become worse. By ground and air, the UN claimed to have delivered more than 700,000 metric tons of food to Bosnians during the war. However, in Sarajevo and Hrasnica, only a small amount of food reached the people, and it was of poor quality. For example, for four or five people in a family for a day, you would get some beans that could be held in one hand, or some rice, or a can with very fatty meat in it called decar. Older people and some younger people got sick from that meat. Often, you got biscuits, and I saw the date on them was 1973. The biscuits were older than I! If someone had told me that the UN gave us 20-year-old biscuits, I wouldn't have believed them. The biscuits were like stones. People couldn't eat them. We ground them down and made cakes. The UN rarely gave us oil or sugar. Because of the food situation, some people got sick, and some died.

Many more people would starve if they relied only on UN assistance. Fortunately, people were united. Neighbor helped neighbor. The haves helped the have-nots.

Humanitarian aid organizations also helped.

In Sarajevo, the situation was worse because it was almost surrounded, and the only way to get out and back for most citizens was to go through the tunnel under the airport.

To get food, I decided to walk west on the "Road of Death" over Mount Igman to the town of Pazaric. Pazaric was under Bosnian control, and Muslim farmers lived there. They had tons of food but no flour.

My mother was worried about my trip. "The Serbs regularly

shell the 'Road of Death.' Be careful," she said. "Try to stay in wooded areas so they can't see you. Stay away from clearings."

"I'll be careful and come back soon," I responded.

I collected 1.3 cubic yards of wood and exchanged it for around 40 pounds of flour. In Pazaric, I would exchange that flour for around 40 pounds of potatoes. Back in Hrasnica, those potatoes would be exchanged for around 90 pounds of flour. We made the flour into bread. Bread was the main meal we ate, and our family used up around 70 pounds of flour in only seven or eight days. I felt exhausted collecting that wood, but not doing it meant starvation.

It was decided that Amir and I would go to Pazaric separately, and I would go first. I put the flour in my rucksack and started walking on the "Road of Death" at around 3 a.m. The dirt road was level at first and then rose upward as it climbed the mountain.

I saw other Bosnians walking on the road. Some were going to and from Pazaric with food. I also saw Bosnian soldiers and people going to other places in Bosnia.

Wreckage of cars and trucks dotted the sides of the road, destroyed by Serbian shells. Vehicles moving on that road were a popular target. People walking on the road were not shelled as often because they were harder to see.

I saw trucks traveling on that road; most of them were bringing humanitarian aid to Sarajevo. The Chetniks shelled some of them. When that happened, the drivers pulled off the road and stopped until the shelling ended. The less brave drivers got out and hid during the shelling. Whenever a truck came near us, we hid so we wouldn't be hit by shrapnel if the vehicle was attacked. (Trucks also brought humanitarian aid to Sarajevo through Serbian-held roads. But the Chetniks confiscated much of that aid and harassed the truck drivers.)

At the top of the mountain, I went through small villages.

From one of them, I looked down. Because I was so high up, I could see Sarajevo and the towns around Mount Igman. All the places the Chetniks controlled had electricity and were lighted, and all the places controlled by us had no electric power and were dark. It was a strange sight.

As I kept going, my heart beat faster, and I couldn't breathe. I kept stopping to catch my breath. This had never happened to me before. I thought the reason was because I never before walked on a mountain for this long and wasn't used to it.

I walked down the mountain and arrived in Pazaric after eight hours. Pazaric had many farm houses, and I knocked on the door of one of them.

In Hrasnica, we had tried to farm the land between the buildings, but it wasn't good. There were too many bricks and too much sand in the dirt. My mother grew a small amount of beans and tomatoes in a garden behind our apartment building. It helped a little. Here, the land was rich and fertile. I saw cows, milk, cheese, many varieties of vegetables, and warehouses full of potatoes.

I exchanged the flour for potatoes and walked back over Mount Igman. There were no problems on the way back except for my heart beating fast and the difficulty catching my breath.

Since my trip to Pazaric was such a success, Amir went there immediately, and afterwards we both made regular trips.

When the shelling got too severe on the "Road of Death," I walked on another trail. However, that trail took much longer, and I preferred not to take it.

Amir and I went back to our position near Siljak. Between guarding the front line, our brigade collected wood. The winter was coming fast. We had to pull the trees on the ground like horses because we didn't have trucks to carry them. While walking on the trail to get wood, I felt pains in my chest. On the road to Pazaric, I could stop, but here I couldn't because other soldiers couldn't pass me on the narrow trail. The pain in my chest got worse. I knew something was wrong but said nothing. I hoped the problem would disappear if I ignored it. Wasn't I too young to have anything serious?

Another winter arrived. I always liked to watch snow falling on the ground and finally see the surface become white. However, sitting outside in a snow-filled, freezing trench wasn't fun. The snow kept coming and covered the ground. It didn't care if I was inside watching it or outside sitting in it.

It was my brother's turn to be in the cabin, but he decided to stay with me outside. It was so cold that we stayed near a big container which burned wood and was used as a heater. Even that wasn't enough. We had to jump up and down and rub our bodies.

We heard a noise behind us, and three soldiers in camouflaged white uniforms appeared. Two were in their early thirties, and the other one was about 40.

"Hello. Where's the commander, Jepa?" the older one asked us.

"He's somewhere, but we don't know," I answered. "You should wait for him."

"We're in a hurry. We don't have time to wait. We're scouts and came here to see what's going on with the enemy."

We looked at them for a while.

"In front of our trench is a minefield," I said.

"Do you know where the mines are?"

"No, but Jepa knows," I said. "It would be better if you wait for him."

"He's not here at the moment," Amir said. "Just wait."

They waited for about 15 minutes and then decided to go.

"No, don't do that," I said. "It's not a good idea to cross the minefield without him."

They said they were in a hurry and went downhill. We looked at them until they disappeared in the distance.

Half an hour later, we heard some kind of explosion that sounded like a bullet. It was choked by the snow but loud enough that some snow fell off trees in our surroundings.

"What was that?" Amir asked.

Soon after, one of the younger men came running. He seemed upset and frightened. He told us that one of his friends stepped on a mine and was wounded. They needed our help to move him.

"I told you not to go across the minefield without our commander!" Amir yelled.

"What happened with the third man in your group?" I asked.

"He stayed with the wounded man."

Amir and I hesitated. I was more afraid of being an invalid than of death. However, the wounded man had to be bleeding badly, and time shouldn't be lost.

"Amir, please stay here," I said. "There's no need to risk both our lives. The three of us should be able to bring the wounded man up here by ourselves."

"No, I don't want to listen to you at all! I'm going with you!"

"But Amir..."

"I'm going whether you like it or not!" So we all went.

It look quite a long time to reach the men. We walked in their footsteps because mines weren't under those spots. Even though it was freezing, our faces were covered with sweat. I was terrified.

We finally reached the spot and saw that the other younger man had lost his right foot and was bleeding badly. His foot looked like a cut opened fish. I could see bones, and the bottom of the foot was hanging by a piece of skin. It made me feel sick. The wounded man didn't feel pain. He was frightened. I bandaged his foot, while he smoked a cigarette, trembling and shaking. We carried him out of the minefield, slowly stepping in their footsteps. Sometimes we slipped, and I was afraid we would find another mine. When we got close to our trench, I called to the soldier in the next trench.

"Feka, we have a wounded man here, and we're very tired! Come and help us!"

"Just walk in the footprints!"

"We are, but we need help!"

"I'll get a stretcher and go to your trench!"

We reached our trench where Feka and other soldiers were waiting, and we put him on a stretcher.

"Could anyone give me another cigarette?" the wounded man asked. "I'm so cold." His face was blue, he was shaking, and he said he now felt unbearable pain in his leg but didn't cry. He bore pain well. Someone put a cigarette in his mouth and lit it.

They took him to the hospital, and we went back to the trench.

The days and nights got so cold that we couldn't stay in our trench for long even with the heater. We agreed to keep guard in one hour shifts instead of two. While one of us was on guard, the other would be in our cabin sitting in front of a fire.

It was my turn to keep guard, and I was just about to go out when my brother came in.

"Elvir, don't go. There is no need to freeze. It's so cold and dark out. I don't believe the Chetniks will attack us. For God's sake, it's 2 a.m."

I hesitated and finally decided to listen to him.

"Okay. We'll both stay here but only if we can go out

every fifteen minutes to make sure nobody is in front of the trench. Do you agree?"

He agreed.

As time went by, we felt sleepy and had to talk to keep ourselves awake.

"Elvir, sing me a sevdalinka," Amir said.

"Snow is falling on the blossoms, on the fruit..." I sang, while Amir took his rifle pretending to be a guitarist.

Suddenly, his "guitar" boomed a few times, and I was deafened by the "loud music." The cabin was full of smoke that smelled of powder. Amir accidentally fired his rifle, and bullets from it were embedded in a wall of the cabin.

"Amir, did you hurt yourself?"

"No, I didn't. Are you okay?"

"I'm okay."

We looked at each other with our eyes wide open for a while, and I started to laugh. He laughed with me. I stopped laughing and slapped him across his face.

"Don't do that again!" I shouted.

Amir looked at me strangely without saying a word for a long time. I thought he was angry at me because I slapped him, and I felt so sorry for him because he looked like he would cry at any moment.

"Elvir, the slap you gave me was louder than the gunfire." He smiled, and we both laughed.

Before, the pain in my chest had occurred while I was walking uphill. Now, whether in the trench or in the cabin, the pain came back and stayed with me for a long time. I thought I had a cold or the flu, and it would go away. But it got worse. When a shell came over my head, I didn't hear it. I just heard my heart beating in my ears.

When we went to the rear to do chores, I felt tired. While

the other soldiers could go up hills easily, I was far away in the rear.

Something was wrong, but I refused to accept it. I didn't tell anyone about my problems.

CHAPTER EIGHT

WE JOIN THE INVALID UNIT

The beginning of the new year 1994 found us still freezing near Siljak. Amir was in the trench, and Jepa and another soldier (whose name I don't remember) visited me in the cabin. While we were talking, I felt another pain in my chest that got worse. I couldn't breathe and thought I would die. Jepa and the soldier stared at me.

"What's going on?!" Jepa yelled. "Your mouth changed color!"

Finally, the pain went away, and I began to breathe normally.

"What's going on?" Jepa asked.

"I don't know. I think I have the flu."

"You don't have the symptoms of the flu," the soldier said "You must see a doctor immediately."

"I'll write a pass for you to see a doctor," Jepa said. "You'll leave immediately. Other soldiers will take your place in the trench."

"But I feel..."

"I just gave you an order," Jepa interrupted.

I explained the situation to my brother, left the front line, and went to a doctor, a general practitioner. He listened to my heart and measured my blood pressure. He said nothing but kept shaking his head. He sent me to an internist.

The internist also listened to my heart, measured my blood pressure, and attached me to an EKG machine.

"You have cardiac arrhythmia and very high blood pressure for someone your age," he said.

"What's cardiac arrhythmia?"

"It's an abnormal heart beat."

"What's the cause of it?"

He didn't answer and sent me to see a cardiologist in Kosevo Hospital in the northeast part of Sarajevo. My journey there began at the entrance of the tunnel that ran under the Butmir Airport. Because wounded and ammunition were constantly traveling through the tunnel, the police told me to come back the next day, which I did. This time, they told me to wait. Since it was icy cold, I made a fire and kept putting wrapping paper and trash into it.

Some children (aged around 10 and 11) came by and sat around the fire. They didn't bother me until they crowded close to the fire, and none of its warmth reached me.

"Go away!" I yelled at them. "Make your own fire!" I'm afraid I sounded mean.

They left but came back again. Again, they blocked the fire's warmth from me.

"Go away!" I yelled again.

They left but approached me again. "We're cold," one of them said.

"Can't you make your own fire?"

"We like your fire."

"You can stay but don't get in front of me." They did that. As I warmed my hands, I felt ashamed that I chased those poor children. I vowed I would never grow mean like my father. I also laughed because the situation was somewhat humorous.

After three hours, I finally went through the tunnel and made my way across the bomb-damaged city. I walked most of the way. Sometimes, trams brought me short distances. The conductor said they couldn't travel more because they would be shelled. A few times, I heard explosions and gunshots.

It took between seven and eight hours to reach Kosevo Hospital. The hospital and areas around it were badly damaged by shells. Like other hospitals in Sarajevo, it had been deliberately targeted.

Before the war, Kosevo Hospital boasted 41 clinics, 2,100 beds, and the most modern medical equipment. Located only 660 yards from the front line, it was shelled severely, particularly at the beginning of the war, and many clinics were completely destroyed. Electricity, gas, oil, water, medical supplies, and medicines were rationed. Often, people needing operations had to bring fuel to run the generators and water to sterilize the instruments. Patients died because they didn't have fuel for their respirators.

After waiting for hours in a crowded waiting room, I saw a doctor and had an EHO (which is similar to a MRI or CAT scan) taken of my body. Then I met with a cardiologist who examined the EHO.

"You have a congenital abnormality on the atrium of your heart," he said. "You have a hole five millimeters and an aneurysm two and a half centimeters."

I hadn't reached 20 and had all these medical problems. I felt tears coming to my eyes.

"How could I have all these problems?" I asked through my tears. "I'm only eighteen."

"They're congenital. You were born with them."

"What's an aneurysm?"

"An abnormal dilation of a blood vessel."

126

"How could I have a hole in my heart? I don't understand that."

The doctor briefly explained my condition. The heart has four chambers, the left and right atriums and the left and right ventricles. Unoxygenated blood reaches the right atrium and flows into the right ventricle. The heart contracts and pumps it into the lungs, where the blood becomes oxygenated and goes back to the heart. That oxygenated blood reaches the left atrium, flows into the left ventricle, and the heart pumps it to the rest of the body. A wall called the septum separates the right atrium and right ventricle from the left atrium and left ventricle. I had a hole in that wall between the atriums called Atrial Septal Defect. Because of that hole, oxygenated blood was mixing with unoxygenated blood, and the heart was stressed during severe physical activity and had to work harder.

"What's the treatment?" I asked.

"The best treatment is that the hole should have been closed when you were four years of age."

"It's too late for that. I'll soon be nineteen."

"Yes, the hole might have to be repaired in the future. Because of the war, we're unable to do any heart operations of that kind now, and we don't have medicines to give you because of shortages. You'll have to wait for the end of the war to do any of that. In the meantime, I'll have to write a note to the army commission that you're not able to go up hills because of your medical condition."

I was shot at and shelled many times, but bullets and shrapnel never touched me. Now, a heart disease I was born with would ruin my life. I found a quiet spot and cried.

I believed in a person's destiny. Perhaps it was my destiny to have Atrial Septal Defect and find out about it during the war at the front. But I couldn't understand the reason for it.

At army headquarters in Hrasnica, a commission of several officers and doctors looked through my medical documents. They talked amongst themselves and looked at me.

"Because of your condition, you're not to go up hills, and because soldiers have to walk up hills, you can't be in a regular unit," the head of the commission said. "We'll give you a choice. You can serve in a special unit in a trench and not be obliged to go up hills. Or you'll be a moral support for the war and be in a secure place behind the lines."

Being in a trench was dangerous, but I wanted to be part of the effort to end the siege of Sarajevo.

"I'll take the first option and be in a trench."

"Then you'll serve with the invalid unit."

"What about my twin brother Amir? We served together in Bijela kosa and Siljak. I want him to serve with me in the invalid unit."

"Does your brother also have a medical condition that keeps him from going up hills?"

"No."

"We can't have able bodied soldiers serving in the invalid unit. You'll have to go without him."

"We promised to stay together throughout the war. I want us to serve together."

"You're not in a position to make such orders!" he yelled. "You'll go to the invalid unit alone, and that's an order! Refusing an order is insubordination and punishable by imprisonment! Dismissed!"

Without another word, I walked away.

When I told my parents about my medical condition and the refusal of the commission to let Amir serve in the invalid unit with me, they took the news calmly.

"After the war, you'll see a doctor again," my father said. "As to the decision of the commission, you can't refuse an order."

"No, but perhaps you can get the order changed," my mother said. "Mido Botulja might be able to help you. He's a friend of the family and owes us a favor."

Mido Botulja was a lawyer before the war. During the war, he had a high position in the army. He still had an office in a building in Hrasnica, and I went there.

Mido was wearing an officer's uniform and sitting behind a desk in his office. After I explained my problem, he thought for a moment, looked in a book, and wrote something on a paper.

"There was a law in the former Yugoslavia that twins shouldn't be separated in the army if they don't want to be," he said. "I'm writing a note that gives the details of this law and says that you and Amir should stay together." He handed me the note. "Give this note to the commission."

At army headquarters, each officer and doctor of the commission slowly read the note and spoke amongst themselves. I heard the name "Mido Botulja" mentioned several times. That name seemed to be more important than the law.

"This commission has decided that Elvir Kulin and Amir Kulin will serve in the invalid unit together," the head of the commission said without looking at me. "They are to report to it immediately."

I was overjoyed that Amir and I would be together. When he arrived at our flat, I told him the good news and asked if he objected being in an invalid unit when he was physically fit. He was also happy we would be together.

Amir had had heart pains before the war and suspected he had Atrial Septal Defect too because it's a genetic condition. He kept asking me to tell him my symptoms to see if he had similar ones. We had different problems. He could go up hills without difficulty.

"I may not have Atrial Septal Defect, but I have some problem with my heart," he said. "If the pains don't go away, I'll have to see a doctor after the war."

Because the pains continued after the war, Amir got an EHO scan of his heart. It showed a minor heart valve defect. The doctor said an operation wasn't advised or necessary.

The invalid unit or the fifth cheta was stationed in the bottom of the eastern part of Mount Igman in a place called Stojcevac. (See Map Two.) Its objective was to keep the Chetniks from capturing Mount Igman again.

I had heard of this unit before. It consisted mostly of people who were wounded, but there were many people who were sick or had had complicated operations before the war. Because of their health, they weren't able to go up hills or carry heavy equipment. Other soldiers made jokes about them such as: "If those people are unable to take care of themselves, how can they defend a trench?" However, since invalids can't retreat, they would defend their positions for a longer time. Because of that, I thought that Stojcevac was more secure than the other trenches.

Hrasnica was much closer to Stojcevac than to Bijela kosa. It only took Amir and me a half hour to walk there, and we didn't have to walk over Mount Igman. (Because trucks going to and from Stojcevac were constantly shelled, Amir and I never rode on them. We walked there and back throughout the war.)

As we walked through Stojcevac, we heard gunfire that sounded louder as we got closer to the front line. The buildings we passed were badly damaged by shells. There was a large shell-damaged house called Titova Vila (in English: Tito's Villa). Next to it were smaller buildings where officers had their offices. We were directed to an office in one of those buildings and reported to a uniformed commander named Saba. To my surprise, he seemed only five years older then I. We introduced ourselves and told him about our situation.

"Not far from us is the front line," Saba said. "Even though we don't attack the Chetniks, they shell and shoot at us on a regular basis, and we have had casualties. Just before you arrived, a soldier named Zeka was badly wounded when a shell exploded high above him in a tree. We have a shortage of weapons and ammunition, so only shoot if the Chetniks attack or if you have a clear shot."

Saba walked to the door. "Let's introduce you to some of the soldiers in our unit," he said. We walked to Titova Vila.

Titova Vila was one of Tito's former residences and used by the militia and the army. It was closed to the public while Tito was alive. After Tito died, it was open to the people and became a restaurant. Because it was located near the front line, it became vacated during the war.

We went into the building and walked to where some soldiers were sitting on damaged chairs and couches. Most of the soldiers were old, but some were young and disabled.

Most weren't in uniform. Since I was shy, I wondered how they would accept me. I imagined them to treat us the same way as the soldiers in Bijela kosa did, being unfriendly or offensive and playing jokes on us because we were novices. I soon realized I was wrong.

"Soldiers, let me introduce our two novices," Saba said. (Even though we were in an army unit before this, we were new to this unit and considered novices.)

The soldiers stood up and smiled.

"Merhaba," I said, as did my brother.

"Merhaba," they greeted us in unison and started approaching us so that one by one, they could introduce themselves and shake hands with us. Their expressions told me that most of them were cheerful, friendly, sociable, and nice to talk with.

Most of them looked confused and seemed to be wondering why we were attached to their unit. Amir and I were the youngest people there and seemed healthy.

"What's the main reason why you're attached to this unit?" someone asked us.

"I have a congenital abnormality in my heart that prevents me from going up hills," I said. "My brother is with me because in the army, twins shouldn't be separated."

"That's too bad about your heart," another of them said. The others agreed.

That day, Saba handed Amir and me automatic rifles, and he took us to the front line. We ran through a field, hid behind a tree, and then ran behind another obstacle. Then we ran to the trench and jumped into it.

The front consisted of a very long, continuous trench. Between it and the Chetnik trench was a stream (where ducks paddled in) and a minefield.

There were no earth cabins. Part of the trench was straight, and part was curved. Because trees were sparse, soldiers had to walk to the trench at night or run to the trench during the day. Behind part of our trench were the remains of a tire store. There was a hole in its ceiling, and outside were destroyed and burned tires.

We walked through the trench and were introduced to the soldiers. Like the soldiers in Titova Vila, most didn't have uniforms and seemed to be friendly. As we walked, we heard sporadic rifle and machine gun fire. As in Bijela kosa and Siljak, most of it was from Chetnik side.

Saba assigned us to a space in the trench far from the other soldiers. Amir and I looked quickly over the top of it. The Chetnik trench was level with ours, and there was a large hill in the distance called Golo Brdo. The Chetniks had a sniper position on it.

Saba explained that soldiers usually kept guard in the trench for two hours. Then, they were relieved and stayed at Titova Vila for two hours. Sometimes, when the bombing became intensive, they stayed in the trench for eight hours. After a few months, they were sent home for a week. When there was a cease-fire, they were sent home sooner.

"Sometimes you'll hear the Chetniks, but don't get into a conversation with them," Saba said. "Even in an innocent conversation, important military information could slip out. To prevent that from happening, just don't talk to them."

We heard more gunfire and shelling.

"I know that some commanders from other sectors are also black marketeers and shoot at the Chetniks during the day and trade supplies with them at night," Saba said. "Forget about doing that here. If you meet with the Chetniks for whatever reason, you'll go to jail."

Saba walked away, and I looked around. This trench looked similar to World War I trenches I had seen photos of.

It got dark. From the Chetnik trench, we heard drunken singing. They stopped their singing and shot their rifles intensively at our trench while cursing at us. Scared, Amir and I got down lower. I heard bullets whining above us. One of the soldiers in our trench picked up his rifle, stood up, aimed at the Chetnik trench, and shot a bullet at them. The Chetniks cursed, stopped their shooting, and kept quiet all night.

As the days passed, we learned the shelling patterns of the Chetniks opposing us. They shelled us intermittently. The shelling was more intensive here than in Bijela kosa or Siljak because there were fewer trees, and our trenches were easier to see. Because of that, more of our soldiers were wounded by shrapnel. The shells were mostly the same calibers as they used in Bijela kosa and Siljak. Fortunately, none of their shells landed in our trench. Also, machine gun and rifle fire were often heard, mostly from the Chetnik side. The Chetniks were well hidden, so we could never see them. But we heard them talking amongst themselves. Often, they cursed at us, and we cursed at them.

Each night in Stojcevac was a repetition of the night before. The Chetniks got drunk in their trench and shot intensively at us. When a soldier on our side shot a bullet at them, they would then keep quiet.

After a heavy rain, the trench was filled with water. During that time, we had to sit in mud and water. This was very difficult, partly because according to Islam, it's forbidden for Muslims to be dirty. Islam requires physical and spiritual cleanliness. In the physical aspect, Muslims must clean their bodies, clothes, homes, and communities and are rewarded by God for doing so.

When the trench was filled with water during a cease-fire, we sat or lay on the ground behind the trench and tried to hide behind a bush, a tree or a rise on the ground. We knew we were exposed; the Chetniks often violated cease-fires and might shoot us. But we didn't care.

The Chetniks never exposed themselves, even during a cease-fire when their trench was filled with water. They were more disciplined than we were and would be severely punished if they didn't follow orders from their commander.

The army food in Stojcevac was no better than what we ate in Bijela kosa and Siljak. Here, we usually had beans, potatoes, and water.

Whenever the former President of Yugoslavia Josip Broz Tito had visited different places in Yugoslavia, he had a villa waiting for him. There were many Titova Vilas across Yugoslavia. No hotel suite or a room in someone's house was suitable for the president of a "Socialist Republic." Tito visited Titova Vila in Stojcevac once a year. The building was once beautiful.

It had a basement, two floors, and was constructed of stone and wood. It had a dining room, exercise rooms, a gym, bedrooms, a kitchen, a lounge, and many other rooms. In those rooms were expensive furniture and a grand piano. Surrounding the villa were trees, a garden, and a large fence. What mostly attracted Tito to Titova Vila in Stojcevac was the hunting area in the woods behind it. Tito loved to shoot animals.

When Amir and I stayed at Titova Vila, much of it was ruined. There were shell holes and shell damage all over it, and much of it was burned. Soldiers tore down one side of a wall to remove some of its furniture. Other pieces of furniture were there, but they were burned. There were no windows, and plastic was on the window frames. Soldiers slept, relaxed, ate, and played cards in the rooms that weren't as badly damaged and were the most protected from shells. The Serbs constantly shelled Titova Vila, particularly at night, and explosions were common while I stayed there. The roof of Titova Vila was badly damaged by shells. Soldiers didn't spent much time in its top floors because there was little protection from shrapnel there.

While I slept in Titova Vila, a shell sometimes hit the building. I ignored it, as did the other soldiers. When that happened, I turned on my improvised bed and said, "A shell hit the roof." and went back to sleep. I was told that before I arrived, some soldiers were killed in Titova Vila by a shell hitting the building.

In Stojcevac, soldiers kept guard in pairs and were usually separated from one another by 55 to 110 yards. I couldn't tell how far the Chetnik trench was from our trench, but it was close enough to understand the Serbs when they yelled at us. Amir and I mostly stayed together and kept moving back and forth between the trench and Titova Vila. Sometimes, Saba paired us with other soldiers. The soldiers assigned to me were

Ramiz Durakovic, Gula Merdanovic, and Meho Music. They all were interesting people to talk to. But their behavior was sometimes strange, and I had to adjust to it.

Ramiz Durakovic was tall, wide shouldered, strong, and about 40. He seemed to be arrogant at first, but the more time I spent with him, the more I realized it was not arrogance but self confidence. Ramiz's backbone was damaged from a fall, and he had trouble moving his neck. Whenever he looked around, he had to move his entire body.

"Saba told you not to shoot until the Chetniks attack, or you have a good shot. But sometimes you have to," Ramiz said to me on my first day with him. "Every night, the Chetniks get hold of some alcohol, get drunk in their trench, and shoot at us for a long time. If they're allowed to do that, eventually one of us will get hit. So when that happens, we have to shoot one bullet at them. That scares and quiets them for the rest of the night. Sometimes Saba will check our weapons, and if you're missing too many bullets, he'll get upset. Our brigade doesn't have enough bullets to replace those. So we have to get bullets from elsewhere. We get bullets from another cheta near the Famos sector when we're short, and they get bullets from us when they're short. When we're both short of bullets, we have to be creative and get them from other places."

Ramiz told me about his life. He didn't have an easy childhood. When he was a child, his father died, and his mother raised the family. Sadly, Ramiz didn't get along with his older brother. He said his brother humiliated him and called him a stupid guy. Therefore, Ramiz's mother was the whole family to him: mother, father, and brother.

Ramiz's wife was a Croat. Many times, he talked about her and their relationship. Before the war, Ramiz worked as a shop assistant at a textile store called "Vartex." There, he met his wife who also worked there. She was 10 years younger than he.

Ramiz and his wife had a tough life. They didn't have enough money to buy a flat. So they rented, often moving from one building to another. Finally, just before the war began, they got the money together and bought one.

When the war started, Ramiz's wife fled to Croatia with their two children to live with relatives. At first, she helped Ramiz by sending him food, supplies, and money. They kept in contact by radio transmitter. However later, she stopped contacting him that way.

The Sarajevian post office was destroyed early in the war, and no mail reached us. That changed in 1993 when letters were exchanged by UN aircraft through an organization called the Council of Europe. This was the new way that Ramiz and his wife corresponded. At first, her letters came weekly, then twice a month, and then once a month. Ramiz was upset and concerned about that.

"Something is going on with her," he said.

"What does she say in her letters?" I asked.

"Nothing, and that disturbs me too. If she's having problems, she should mention that in her letters instead of sending them infrequently. Something is happening. I wish she had stayed in Bosnia. We could work out our problems together. When she lives so far away, I feel so helpless."

When Ramiz heard that his wife's boss was assisting her financially, he became suspicious of his motivations and wanted to visit her in Croatia. But our army wouldn't let him leave while the war was going on. If our troops caught him trying to go to Croatia without permission, he might be sent to prison or shot as a deserter, and if the Chetniks caught him, he might be sent to one of their camps or shot as a spy. So Ramiz had to stay and wait.

Gula Merdanovic was 55 and energetic. He didn't act like a man of his age and spent his time with younger people. He didn't like to gossip behind someone's back, liked to tell jokes, and was friendly. I liked him very much and found him comforting to talk to. Gula was here because he was too old and had diabetes. He liked to touch a person's nose with his finger. When I first met him, I saw his finger heading for my face and backed off.

"What are you doing?" I asked surprised.

"I want to touch your nose. I like to touch the noses of people I like," he explained.

"Okay, touch my nose, but don't poke me in the eye."

I held my face as still as possible. Gula touched my nose and laughed.

Gula spoke about his childhood. He was born in Sarajevo. When he was a child at the end of the World War II, Tito's partisans pushed the German army out of Sarajevo. Because he was too young, Gula didn't remember much about his experiences during the war. He knew that some of family were killed by the Germans, and some died from diseases such as the flu. However, Gula's memories after the war were painfully clear. He and his family were poor, and Gula was insulted by children from richer families.

"My parents were unskilled factory workers," Gula said. "Despite what the government said about Yugoslavia being a 'Socialist State' and a 'Workers Paradise,' they received very little pay. We didn't have enough money for food and clothes. The clothes we had were worn out and ripped. Other children were in a better situation, particularly those whose parents were professionals, government officials, or in the military. Of course, they all were Communist Party members. You couldn't get ahead without being a party member. Those children insulted me because I was poor. They hit me and played jokes on me. I remember when something was stolen, they blamed me because I was poor, and people believed them."

Before our war, Gula was a factory worker. Even though he didn't have a university education, he was very knowledgeable, and we spoke about interesting subjects. Gula said he was divorced and didn't have any children.

Meho Music was about 40, short, had dark hair and a smooth baby face. He had been interned in a detention camp called Heliodrom, under the control of the HVO, the Bosnian Croat paramilitaries. Because of Meho's experiences in Heliodrom being beaten and tortured, he had post traumatic syndrome and was declared "unfit" to serve in other units. His main problem was his constant crying. Also, he would suddenly get angry for no apparent reason and yell and curse. Fortunately most of the time, Meho was friendly and easy to talk to.

How Meho ended up in Heliodrom was a long and interesting story. Meho's father owned a chain of grocery stores and was wealthy. Because everything was handed to him, Meho was spoiled, didn't work, and just went to clubs and parties.

"My father got tired of my attitude and ordered me to leave the house without giving me any money," Meho said. "At first, I thought he was joking. But he pushed me out and threatened to call the militia if I returned. I had to make money in a short time, so I got a job as a taxi driver. I kept expecting my father to take me back or give me money, but he didn't."

However, later Meho's father lent him money to open a bakery called "Igmansanska Roso." Meho's bakery was successful, and it became one of the biggest bakeries here. (I went to that bakery before the war and remembered seeing Meho there.) Meho became a rich man and lived in Hrasnica with his wife and son.

In the beginning of our war, Meho drove to Croatia to get flour for his store. On the way, in Herzegovina (a region in southern Bosnia), his truck was stopped by the Croatian army and the HVO. They asked for his identification. When they

realized he was a Muslim business leader, they took him to Heliodrom and took possession of his truck.

Heliodrom is the Bosnian word for heliport, and Heliodrom was a former heliport located a few miles south of Mostar,
the largest city in Herzegovina, located southwest of Sarajevo.
Some prisoners were kept in former helicopter hangars, and
others lived in barracks. Meho was in a barracks. Meho only
saw male prisoners at the camp.

Meho refused to call Heliodrom a detention camp. He
called it a death camp. It was hot and sunny in Herzegovina,
and prisoners got thirsty doing difficult jobs such as building
fences and barracks. However, the Croatian guards wouldn't
give them water, and they had to urinate into a container and
drink it. The Croats also didn't feed them, and they had to eat
grass like cows. That made Meho crazy.

Croat guards tortured Meho with electrical shocks. They
tied him down to the metal frame of a couch and shocked him
until he was unconscious. Meho also saw them torture, beat,
and shoot other prisoners.

Croat guards also put the barrels of their guns into Meho's
mouth and threatened to shoot him. After doing that several
times, Meho got crazy and dared them to pull the trigger. They
didn't.

After many days of such torture, Meho prayed to God to
end his life and provoked armed Croat guards to shoot him.
They didn't.

Meho said the slimmer, weaker prisoners were kept in
the death camp, and the stronger prisoners were sent into the
battlefield to dig trenches at the front. Some of those prisoners
were killed by both sides during the fighting.

When Meho talked about the brutality of the guards,
he cried and cried. Often, I couldn't deal with his crying and
changed the subject.

Meho's wealth saved his life at Heliodrom. He paid the Croat guards to protect him. They didn't give him difficult activities and didn't beat him as much as they did to the other prisoners. Finally, Meho paid money to the camp's administrators to get them to release him. He was exchanged for Croatian prisoners from our camps.

When Meho came back to Hrasnica, he found out that his wife and son were well and still living in Hrasnica. However, the Bosnian army took control of his bakery and used it to feed the troops.

We weren't sure if the HVO guards would be held accountable for their crimes because the Croatian army was fighting the Serbs. We were wrong. After the war, Croatians along with Serbs and Muslims were tried at the UN War Crimes Tribunal at The Hague in the Netherlands.

In regard to Heliodrom, some Bosnian Croats were prosecuted. In March 2000, Mladen Naletilic nicknamed "Tuta" and Vinko Martinovic nicknamed "Stela" were taken into custody at the UN War Crimes Tribunal. Both men were Bosnian Croat paramilitary commanders and charged with 22 counts of murder, beating, torture, plunder, and displacement of thousands of Muslims in the Mostar area. The indictment stated that between April 1993 and January 1994, Muslim civilians and prisoners of war were interned in Heliodrom and another detention camp called Vinko Skrobo where they were repeatedly tortured by Naletilic, Martinovic, and their subordinates. The indictment also stated that during the Bosnian Croatian attack on Mostar, prisoners from Heliodrom were forced by both men to walk in front of the advancing Croatian troops and be human shields. When Mostar was captured, it was "ethnically cleansed" by HVO troops, and prisoners from Heliodrom were forced to remove the corpses from the streets. After a trial in March

2003, Natetilic was sentenced to 20 years, and Martinovic was sentenced to 18 years .

Even though the brutality of Serbian detention camps was known to the world, Croatian authorities operated similar kinds of camps. Deaths in those camps were mostly caused by starvation, beating, and shooting of individuals.

The Bosnian authorities also ran detention camps, but the prisoners there weren't starved, beaten, or shot. Most were forced to work in agricultural fields.

In Sarajevo and Hrasnica, Serbs were arrested for trying to escape to Serb-controlled areas. Women, children, and the elderly were released. However, the men were held in prisons in Sarajevo and Hrasnica where some were exchanged for Muslim prisoners from Serbian detention camps and prisons. Several 100 prisoners were exchanged each year by both sides.

In the Ramiz Salin Military Prison in Sarajevo, the Central Sarajevo Prison, and other prisons throughout Bosnian controlled areas, Serbian prisoners reported being beaten, poorly fed, and forced to dig trenches on the front line.

I knew about a basement in a department store on Igmanska Street in Hrasnica where Serbs and Muslim soldiers were imprisoned. The Serbs were fifth columnists, secretly hid weapons in their homes, or radioed messages to the Chetniks. They were kept in the basement prison for the war's duration or exchanged for Muslim prisoners. The Muslim soldiers were held in the prison for days or weeks for minor military offenses. The Muslims and Serbs were separated to keep them from fighting each other. No Serb was beaten, tortured, or killed in this prison. However, most Serbs were beaten in their homes by Muslim police when captured.

At Titova Vila, I met another interesting soldier named Hasan Pinjo. He was in Stojcevac because he was in his sixties and too old to serve in a regular unit. He was rude, yelled at people, but I liked his stories. Hasan said he worked in Germany, killed a Turkish man there, and went to prison for it. The German authorities deported him back to Bosnia, and he went to prison here. When the war started, he was let out to join the army.

"They let you out of prison even though you committed a murder?" I asked him doubtfully.

"Are you saying I'm a liar?" he asked. "Making such statements can get a person killed. The Bosnian army needed every available man to fight in the war, and I proved I can kill a person."

People said that Hasan hunted in the woods for animals. I heard a shot and saw a dead duck on the ground near Hasan. He shot it, and I was furious.

"How could you shoot that duck?!" I yelled. "It was innocent!"

"It flew near me, so I shot it! It's just a duck!"

"Isn't there enough killing in this war for you?!" I walked away and decided to stay away from Hasan.

Hasan Pinjo didn't go back to prison after the war. I discovered that he was driving a bus.

The medic in Stojcevac was a guy named Izo. Soldiers ridiculed and imitated him because he didn't know too much about medicine and wasn't qualified for his position. For example, when a soldier was badly wounded, Izo panicked, got confused, and put the bandages on that person clumsily.

I was told that a wounded and unconscious person shouldn't be put on his back or he might swallow his saliva or tongue and choke. Such a person should be put on his stomach or side. But Izo kept laying wounded and unconscious soldiers on their backs. Also, when a soldier was wounded in his back, four people were needed to move that person, or it might cause him more injuries. But Izo tried to move a back injured soldier by himself.

One time, a soldier named Smoki was scratched by a bullet. The hit area was red and bruised, but Smoki wasn't bleeding. Izo covered the bruised area with many bandages while we watched, smiling at his stupidity.

I don't know how Izo got his position. I heard he wanted to escape from the front line and tried to remain in the rear for as long as possible.

Everybody in the invalid unit was a Muslim with one exception, a Gypsy. His name was Mujo. Guarding a building, he was shot in the shoulder by a Serbian sniper early in the war and couldn't move his arm. Most of the other soldiers refused to keep guard with him because in Bosnia, Gypsies had a reputation for being dirty, begging for money, being illiterate, not respecting the law, and not wanting to work. However, Mujo was a decent, responsible person who respected other people. He was also clean and took baths in a nearby spring even during the winter when the water was freezing.

Because Gypsies didn't register babies when they were born, they didn't have identities and couldn't apply for a job, go to school, or go to a doctor. Therefore, life for them was difficult. They also couldn't be mobilized to join the army, and I was surprised to see one here.

Our commander, Saba, also had interesting stories about his life and how he ended up in Stojcevac. Saba was in the Yugoslavian army before the war in Bosnia started. When the war began, Saba's Yugoslavian army unit was sent to occupy Foca. Because Saba was a Muslim, he was cursed at and insulted by Serbs in his unit. When he saw Chetniks burn down a house in which Muslims inside were burnt alive, Saba decided he couldn't be part of that army. He defected, joined the Bosnian army and fought against the Yugoslavian army in the Grebak area.

"It felt strange to be fighting the troops I previously served with. But I didn't belong with them anymore," he said. "Outnumbered by the Yugoslavian tanks and artillery, we fell back. Finally, we made our way to Hrasnica."

Saba and his family lived in Foca, and his parents left Foca when war began. They went to Gorazde, Sarajevo, Croatia, and finally to Turkey. Saba helped other relatives join small groups who were escaping from the town. Most of them went to Europe, but some were killed by the Chetniks.

Because of his knowledge of weapons, Saba was appointed commander of our unit even though he was only 25 years old at the time. Like the rest of us in this unit, Saba was disabled. He had had two major backbone operations and couldn't run or go uphill.

In Stojcevac, most of the buildings near the front line were people's houses. Most of the families who lived in those houses were evacuated to Hrasnica. Usually, the oldest male in a family stayed behind and guarded the house from looters. One of those males had the last name of Botula. He was a Muslim and in his eighties. Botula prayed loudly to God five times a day. Every day in the trench, just before the sun came up, I heard him praying. The Chetniks must have heard him too, and I wondered why they didn't completely destroy his house by shell fire. Some shells landed on Botula's house or near him while he prayed. But he didn't panic or run away. He ignored the shells without a trace of fear on his face and patiently finished his prayers. I admired his courage and devotion.

The commander ordered civilians near the front line to put curtains on their windows so the Chetniks wouldn't see the lights. Even though Botula's house was near the front line, he refused to listen to that order and put candles in his window without a curtain.

Botula noticed me watching him and invited me inside his house. I told him I could hear him praying in our trench, and the Chetniks could probably hear him too.

"I know the Chetniks can hear me. I want them to hear me," he said. "This is my act of defiance against what they are doing to the Muslims in Bosnia."

"Aren't you afraid of a shell hitting you?"

"If I'm to be killed or wounded by a shell, it is God's will."

"I also believe in a person's destiny," I said. "But why tempt fate?"

"I'm an old man," he said. "My life will soon be over. I can afford to tempt fate. At least I'll die being faithful to my religion and my country."

I visited Botula a few more times, and he told me about his life. During World War II, when Yugoslavia was occupied, German soldiers appeared in his neighborhood from time to time. Most of the time, they acted politely toward Muslims and didn't give them difficulties. It was a different story when the Ustasha appeared. They took young Muslims to Sarajevo; some of those returned, and some were hanged. Botula cried because he knew some of the people who were killed. Near the end of the war, Botula joined Tito's partisans and went to the Krajina region of Bosnia. He took part in several battles there. He said the partisans were always short of food and clothes, and some partisans died of diseases such as the flu and typhus.

Botula also told me about Muslim dating customs when he was younger. In the 1990s, Bosnian Muslim men and women could be seen together, touching and holding one another. But in the 1930s, such a sight was improper and embarrassing, and the woman involved was considered to be a prostitute. It was forbidden for a man and woman to be close in public with their arms around each other. When they danced, a couple couldn't touch each other; they had to just hold the same piece of cloth. A man was allowed only one girlfriend, but a woman could have many boyfriends. Men often met women by throwing pebbles at their windows, and this was how Botula sometimes met women. He dated many Muslim women and had a high opinion of them. During World War II, people became more tolerant of each other, and many Muslim dating customs were relaxed.

Chapter Nine

THE SIEGE CONTINUES

On February 5, 1994, a 120 millimeter mortar shell exploded in a crowded outdoor marketplace called "Markale" in Sarajevo in the Old Muslim Town, killing 67 people and wounding around 200. It was the worst attack during the siege of Sarajevo. The market was located between two buildings and consisted of steel tables where people bought clothes, appliances, and other items. (I visited the spot after the war and spoke to a woman who witnessed the attack.)

I was home on leave watching television when that shell hit. The electricity had come back shortly before this time, as did the water service. There were no movies or music programs on TV, just news. One of the news stories was about the shell landing at the marketplace. I saw dead bodies, and some didn't have heads. There was a young man on his motorbike, and shrapnel killed him. He was still on his bike but bent over a fence. It was usual to see dead people, but they were usually lying on the ground.

The UN command stated the shell came from Bosnian Serb positions in the mountains to the northeast. Serbian gunners denied they had fired that shell.

US President Bill Clinton first stated there would be no

military retaliation for that mortar attack. However, two days later, under pressure, he stated that NATO would give the Serbs a week to remove their tanks and artillery 12.5 miles from the center of the city. Any heavy weapons found within that area after seven days would be subject to bombing strikes by NATO warplanes.

When Amir and I returned to the front line, it was quiet. The soldiers were sad about the people killed at the marketplace but happy that finally NATO would bomb Serbian artillery and tanks. We hoped to see the fireworks. However, days before the ultimatum expired, the Serbs withdrew their heavy weapons. Karadzic appeared with Russian diplomats and stated that they had accepted a Russian proposal for withdrawal and the sending of Russian troops into some areas left vacant by the Serbs. We were disappointed. NATO threatened to bomb the Serbs many times but never did. Perhaps they never would.

Ramiz had a pack of cards and played card games with other soldiers in Titova Vila. One time, I watched as he and Gula played a card game called pispil, which they played for fun not money.

"Elvir, join us in the game," Ramiz said.

"Yes, please do," Gula said.

I felt shy and wasn't ready to play cards with them. "I can't play cards now."

"Then write the scores on a piece of paper," Ramiz said, which I did.

Gula had more points than Ramiz, and it looked as though he would win the game. As the game progressed, it seemed like Gula was the winner, and Ramiz became angry.

"It's not possible you had such great cards all the time!" Ramiz yelled. "You must have been cheating!"

To be playful, Gula touched Ramiz's nose, but he touched

it too hard. Ramiz's nose went sideways, and his eyes were filled with tears. He was in pain.

"I didn't want to hit you," Gula said. "It was an accident. Please accept my apology."

Ramiz kept quiet, and I thought he would accept Gula's apology. However suddenly, Ramiz stood up and hit Gula several times.

"Now I accept your apology," Ramiz said.

"I didn't want to hit you," Gula repeated.

Ramiz walked away. It was a strange experience to see two adults fighting over a deck of cards and behaving like children.

Ramiz felt sorry he had hit Gula and wished he hadn't done it. Fortunately, Gula didn't hold a grudge against him, and a few days later, I saw them playing cards, talking, and joking again. Gula also touched Ramiz's nose but this time softly.

Meho and I were together in the trench. We kept talking as it got darker. Near us was the stream, and we heard it flowing. In the past, when it got dark, Meho sometimes frightened me by suddenly interrupting our conversation to say that he heard a strange noise. I was always afraid of an attack.

This time, Meho suddenly became quiet and said, "Shhh. I hear something. Someone's coming from the Chetnik position." I kept quiet and listened. After a while, Meho smiled and laughed.

Meho played that trick on me several times. Each time, I believed him but finally realized he was joking. Each time, I didn't say anything, and we continued our conversation. I decided to play a trick on Meho in return.

"Shhh." I said. I acted very serious and forced myself not to laugh. Meho became quiet and listened.

I looked across the field. "I see a man on the ground in between the trenches," I said.

Meho scanned the field. "I don't see anyone." He seemed to believe me.

"If we crawl on the ground in front of our trench, we might see the man. Have your rifle ready. You might need it."

We both crawled on the ground with our rifles for half an hour. I convinced him I saw something. He seemed frightened. Finally, we went back to our trench.

"Where's the man you saw?" Meho whispered.

I smiled and then laughed.

"How could you do that, Elvir?!" Meho yelled. "Fuck you! Fuck you!" Meho then released a storm of more curses at me. He looked as though he was going to hit me but didn't. All the front line heard Meho that night.

Croatian troops attacked and occupied Bosnian territory around the same time that Yugoslavian troops did. Like the Yugoslavian army, the Croatian army soon left the country. Bosnian Croat paramilitary forces occupied their positions and continued the fight.

As early as March 1991, Milosevic and Tudjman agreed to be allies and occupy separate Bosnian territory together, and Croatian forces soon defeated Bosnian army units and controlled 20 percent of Bosnia. Like the Chetniks, Bosnian Croat paramilitaries "ethnically cleansed" Muslims from territories they controlled.

However, soon Bosnian Croat and Bosnian Serb troops fought one another. In July 1992, Croatian and Muslim forces pushed the Chetniks out of Mostar, which the Yugoslavian army had captured in the beginning of the war.

When Mate Boban, the Bosnian Croat nationalist leader, declared the territory that Croatian troops controlled as a separate Croatian republic called "Herzeg-Bosna," fighting broke out in the spring 1993 between Muslim and Croatian troops.

The heaviest fighting took place in Mostar, the proposed capital of Herzeg-Bosna.

In March 1994, under pressure from President Clinton, the Bosnian government, the Croatian government and Bosnian Croatian leaders signed an agreement that linked their territories into one federation. The federation's power would be shared by Bosnian and Croatian leaders, and the president and prime minister would rotate between Bosnians and Croatians. Herzeg-Bosna ceased to exist.

The federation, called the Muslim-Croatian Federation, also meant that Bosnia would have access to the Adriatic Sea and could get weapons and supplies from Croatia. Now, the Bosnian army would have only one enemy to fight, the Bosnian Serbs.

We didn't like the conduct of the Croatians in Bosnia but were practical. The Bosnian Serbs still controlled 70 percent of Bosnia and were still shelling cities. Despite our attacks, that wasn't changing.

With Bosnian and Croatian paramilitaries joining their forces, we expected to hear news about attacks by them. Instead, the Bosnian Serb paramilitaries went on the offensive. In April 1994, using tanks, artillery, and soldiers, they seized the outskirts of Gorazde and began shelling the center of the city. I thought of my cousin Suad in Gorazde and wondered if he was taking part in the fighting.

The UN demanded that the Chetniks pull back from Gorazde. When they didn't, American bombers, flying under NATO command, bombed Serbian military targets around the area for two days, marking the first time NATO airplanes bombed Serbian ground positions in the war. We were very happy and hoped this would be the beginning of an extensive NATO bombing campaign against the Serbs.

After the air strikes, the Serbs stopped their assault but

refused to meet with UN officials. Three days later, they re-started their offensive against Gorazde and captured more of its suburbs. When the Chetniks entered the city limits, NATO warned them that in five days, they would bomb Serbian heavy weapons and other military targets within a 12.5 mile radius of Gorazde's center. At the last moment, the Chetniks withdrew, destroying Gorazde's water treatment facility and burning houses to the ground.

We heard the reason for UN restraint was because Karadzic threatened UN troops in Serbian controlled territory if his troops elsewhere were bombed. That didn't make sense to us. UN troops were armed, trained, and knew the risks when coming here. Because the UN was worried about troops who made the decision to come here, they permitted the killing of Bosnian people. The soldiers agreed with everyone else I spoke with that if UN troops couldn't assist us, they should end the embargo and let us defend ourselves.

It was a rainy day in summer, and Ramiz and I were togeth-er in the trench. Ramiz was going to tell me a story about his childhood. We drank a lot of coffee in the trench, and Ramiz was just about to light a fire to put his coffee pot on.

"When I was..." he began. We heard something buzzing over our heads. We kept quiet, waiting for an explosion, but nothing happened. I felt confused. We looked around but saw nothing.

"Anyway, when I was..." The same buzzing thing flying above interrupted him again.

"What the hell's happening here?" he asked, looking at me with his eyes wide open. The expression on his face made me laugh, and he also laughed. He continued his story.

About 10 minutes later, we heard buzzing again, but this buzz sounded faster than the other buzzes. A long, round object fell near us on the mound of dirt in front of our trench and got half buried in the ground. We looked at it for a while. We saw it was a shell and expected it to explode, but it didn't. Perhaps it had a delayed fuse.

"Ramiz, lie down!" I shouted, and we both got deeper in the trench.

We lay on the ground for a few minutes. Nothing exploded. We stood up and saw Saba approach. "Did you see something unusual on the ground?" he asked.

Ramiz pointed at the object. "You mean this? This shell fell out of the sky without exploding." Saba confirmed that was what he meant.

Saba smiled at us. "Guys, this malyutka came from our positions on Mount Igman." (A malyutka is a Soviet designed anti-tank guided missile.) "I was told this one's motor was broken, couldn't control its route and flew around in circles. It's damaged too much and can't be repaired. I was informed this malyutka might fall in the direction of Stojcevac. I'll have them remove it."

We kept quiet as Saba walked away, and we looked at each other.

"Our artillery sent this missile to us!" Ramiz yelled. "Fuck them!" Ramiz kept cursing the soldiers in charge of our malyutka. "It would be very sad if we were killed by our own artillery," he finally said to me.

I was at home during a shelling of Hrasnica. My mother wasn't in our flat. I knew she was working in our garden and assumed she was coming inside. When she didn't, I ran to the back entrance of my building. She was still watering plants in the garden.

"Shells are falling around us!" I yelled at her. "Come in!"

She looked at me, slowly put down her watering can, and walked in.

"When shells explode nearby, you're to run into our building immediately!" I yelled as soon as she stepped into the building. "What were you waiting for?!"

"I had to water our crops. You need those vegetables to survive. I was just about to finish."

"You can finish watering the plants after the shelling. If you're killed by a shell, the vegetables will not help you. I've seen what a piece of shrapnel can do to a body. Don't delay in coming inside."

After a few more times of a similar experience occurring, I became very worried about her. She seemed to become numb to the shelling. When we were alone in the flat, I expressed my concern.

"It's bad enough worrying that a shell might hit me in the trench," I said. "Now I have to worry about you. What's the problem?"

"The shelling is constant. If I ran inside every time a shelling occurred, I couldn't get any work done. I'm sick of running inside all the time. I'm sick of the shelling."

Before I left for the front, I made my mother promise to come inside immediately each time a shelling occurred. Because I was afraid she wouldn't, I asked my sister to make it a priority. She said she would.

Because Mount Igman's capture would mean that Sarajevo would starve, Stojcevac was considered a very important front and was visited by Bosnian generals and their staffs. They visited Titova Vila and the trenches and said encouraging words to the soldiers. Saba was kept busy saluting and greeting them.

The most notable general who visited was Sefer Halilovic. A former officer in the Yugoslavian army, Halilovic had helped create the Bosnian army when the war started and became its first chief of staff. In 1993, he was in the news for ordering a failed counterattack in the east of Bosnia to free Muslim civilians trapped by Serbian forces. Later, Serbian General Mladic allowed a partial evacuation of those civilians due to UN pressure.

Even though Halilovic was a high ranking officer, the soldiers in Stojcevac didn't treat him so. Because discipline was lax, they didn't salute him or stand at attention in front of him. They treated him like any other soldier. However, after Halilovic walked past them, they stared at his back, impressed that such an important military person would visit.

None of the generals who visited spoke to me except for Fikret Prevljak, the general in charge of our brigade. He showed up at Amir's and my position in the trench at 8 p.m. with two of his aides and Saba. It was quiet at the front. Neither Amir nor I saluted Prevljak because we weren't taught how to salute during our brief army training. Prevljak said, "Merhaba." and asked for our names. We told him. Saba told him we were twins.

"What? Twins shouldn't be together on the front line," Prevljak said. "If a shell lands in this trench, your mother will lose both sons. I want you to be separated."

Amir and I looked at each other. "We refuse to be separated," I said.

"Are you refusing an order from a general?" he asked.

I felt afraid and couldn't talk. Disobeying a general's order could get us into serious trouble. He could have us put into prison for insubordination.

Fortunately, Amir found his voice. "There is a law that twins don't have to be separated in the army if they don't want to be," he said. "Elvir and I are in compliance with that law."

I then explained the story of what we went through to serve together.

156

Prevljak smiled. "If such a law exists, I can't order you to separate. Let's hope shells find other places to land."

"So far, we've been lucky," I said. "Hopefully, our luck will continue."

"Are you frightened?" Prevljak asked, changing the subject.

Amir and I admitted we were, especially when the Chetniks shelled us.

"This is understandable," he said. "Hopefully the shelling should end, and the war will be over soon."

"Yes sir," we said, and they walked down the trench to talk to other soldiers.

Pope John Paul II planned to visit Sarajevo in September but canceled due to threats by Serbian forces. In the weeks preceding the planned visit, shelling and gunfire of Sarajevo increased. Instead, the pope addressed the Sarajevian people by radio and television. I was home during this time with my family, and we heard part of his speech on the radio.

He called on the Serbs, Croats and Muslims to forgive one another. He said, "The spiral or 'wrongs' and 'punishments' will never stop if forgiveness does not come at a certain point."

We weren't impressed by the pope's speech. He was like a teacher, trying to explain to his pupils what's good and what's bad. He didn't say the Chetniks or the Yugoslavian army were the guilty ones for this war. Considering that he held the highest position in the Catholic Church, he could have assumed his position in a better way and appealed to the U.S., UN, NATO, and Russia to stop the war.

Forgiveness was easy for the pope. He lived in a palace in Rome. I lived in a ruined city surrounded by smashed bodies, many of whom were my friends. The pope promised to visit Sarajevo soon but visited Croatia's capital Zagreb instead.

The Bosnian army received new weapons at last and was preparing to attack the Chetniks and try to break the Serbian siege around Sarajevo. The government requested all able bodied men to join the army, and my father joined the commandos. He stood in our flat with a uniform and a helmet.

"I don't know how long I'll be gone," he said to my mother. "Hopefully, the commandos will be push back the Chetniks quickly, and I'll come home soon."

He turned to me. "I'm giving you the same instructions I did when I joined the anti-terrorist force, Elvir. Listen to your mother. Don't disobey her. Do everything she says."

"I'll obey her." Then he left. Again, I was glad after he left and began to breathe easier.

While sitting in the trench with Ramiz and drinking coffee, we heard a voice from the Chetnik trench.

"Hey Muslims, I have a proposal for you!" a Chetnik yelled.

"Let's hear it Serb!" Ramiz yelled back. Nobody was near us, so we didn't worry our conversation would be reported to the commander.

"We have plenty of sugar, vegetables, and cigarettes here!" he yelled. "But we have a shortage of salt and need it!"

"That's interesting!" Ramiz yelled. "We have salt here and need sugar, vegetables, and cigarettes!"

"I suggest you come over here with the salt and exchange it for the stuff we have!"

"I don't like that idea!" Ramiz yelled. "Why don't you come here with the sugar, vegetables, and cigarettes, and we'll give you the salt for it?!"

"If you come here, are you afraid we'll shoot you?! I promise we will not!"

"No, but the order here is that trading supplies with the enemy will land us in prison!" Ramiz yelled. "I can't risk it!"

Another winter arrived in Bosnia, and snow covered the trenches. As in Siljak, we had wood burning heaters. However, like in Siljak, they weren't enough, and we froze and cursed.

Over my mother's objections about my health, I continued to walk on the "Road of Death" on Mount Igman to exchange flour for potatoes in Pazaric. I rested constantly and didn't have problems. However one very cold day, I could hardly catch my breath going there. It took longer getting the potatoes than I planned, and it was getting dark on my way back. There was a dull pain in my chest, and I felt more fatigued the higher I went up the mountain. I kept resting after each 110 yards. Even though it was freezing, I was sweating and thought the cold winter wind was blowing straight through me. My body was shaking and aching with cold.

When I reached Hrasnicki stanovi, a village on Mount Igman, I felt very sleepy and decided to sit down and rest for a while. A few minutes after, my body stopped shaking, and I didn't feel the cold anymore. I closed my eyes and fell asleep.

"Hey, is everything okay with you?" an unknown voice said. The voice didn't seem to be real. I thought I was dreaming but was wrong.

"Get up! Get up!" a man yelled as he shook me. After a few more attempts, he succeeded in waking me. I opened my eyes and saw him. He was carrying a rucksack.

"I'm okay," I said. "Please leave me alone, and let me sleep for a while."

"You can't sleep. You have to get up and walk." He grabbed my hand and practically dragged me down the road. He told me he was also bringing food back from Pazaric and was also a soldier. He was probably in my brigade.

159

Finally, we arrived at my flat, and I went to sleep. Thanks to that man, I didn't freeze to death. Sadly, I never thanked him or got his name.

Chapter Ten

WE PUSH BACK THE CHETNIKS

The year 1995 began with Bosnian army successes. We started to capture territories all over Bosnia controlled by the Serbs. One of those was Mount Vlasic, a large mountain in the center of Bosnia. We didn't think Mount Vlasic could be conquered because there were strong, fortified Chetnik forces there. We launched major attacks against it, but in the beginning each attempt was in vain. Karadzic visited Mount Vlasic a month or so earlier and said it was fortified in the best way, and it wasn't possible to conquer it. In the end, our army proved him wrong.

The Bosnian army decided to attack Mount Vlasic from the other side. It was a vertical cliff, and the Chetniks didn't concentrate weapons on it or expect an attack from that side. Bosnian mountaineers scaled the cliff, captured Mount Vlasic, and the Chetniks fled in panic.

There was a TV transmitter on Mount Vlasic. After our army conquered the mountain, General Mehmed Alagic broadcast from that transmitter. He said, "From now on, the Bosnian TV signal will come from here and will cover a large part of the Republic of Sprska."

Amir and I spent our twentieth birthday, February 6, 1995, in Stojcevac. We were in the trench for much of the day. It was relatively quiet there.

"Happy birthday, Elvir," Amir said.

"Happy birthday," I responded.

This was the extent of our birthday celebrations.

This is our third birthday in the war. I remembered how we had spent our seventeenth birthday just before the war started. Our parents wouldn't allow us to have a big party at home because we would be too noisy and have alcohol. So we celebrated at Pincic's (a woman friend of ours) house. Our friends were there. People played games, sang songs, ate cake, and drank alcohol. But I didn't drink alcohol (and would never drink alcohol) because I knew the effect it had on our father.

In the beginning of May, Croatian tanks, artillery, warplanes, and troops launched Operation Flash, the recapturing of part of the Krajina called western Slavonia. This was territory Croatia had lost to Serbian troops in their 1991 war.

We heard explosions again from Sarajevo. The year before, the Serbs removed some of their heavy artillery around Sarajevo but not all. Now with the artillery they kept, they intensively shelled Sarajevo in retaliation for their recent reverses. At the end of May, a Serbian shell exploded in the main square in Tuzla (a town northeast of Sarajevo), killing 71 people and wounding over 100. NATO began a massive bombing campaign in response to those shellings, and their first targets were ammunition dumps in Pale.

I was on guard in the trench during the night. It was raining, thundering, and lightning.

When morning broke, we went to Titova Vila, and Saba told us the thundering was NATO bombing. At first, we didn't believe him.

"Are you sure that noise was NATO bombing?" Ramiz said.

"I don't believe it," Meho said. Other people agreed with him.

"I was told that NATO bombed Serbian targets last night," Saba said. "They hit ammunition centers in Pale, and many people were killed."

"Then it must be a small, limited bombing," Ramiz said. "NATO will not bomb the Chetniks again."

"I was told this is the beginning of a massive campaign of NATO air strikes."

"I'll believe it when I see it," Ramiz said.

In the beginning of the war, we trusted NATO, but they kept disappointing us. They threatened the Serbs but hardly ever carried out their threats. We thought they would never bomb the Chetniks in a massive way.

In Titova Vila, we heard on the radio that NATO kept bombing other Serb positions around Sarajevo and elsewhere in Bosnia. We said nothing. Some people were still skeptical.

Over the next few days, we heard NATO's bombing and finally believed it. The Serbs were getting what they had been giving to the Bosnian people for three years.

I saw NATO warplanes bomb Serbian positions on Golo Brdo. The British airplanes were high. When they were in front of the target, they suddenly dove, and dropped their bombs. I saw explosions and bullets fired by the Chetniks at them. The soldiers who watched the bombing had smiles on their faces.

NATO also bombed Serbian positions in Hadzici. Because Hadzici was behind part of Mount Igman, I heard the explosions but didn't see them.

In response to the bombing, the Chetniks took 370 UN soldiers hostage and used them as human shields to prevent

NATO from bombing again. Later, those soldiers were released.

The Chetniks began shelling and machine gunning our positions more severely, and some of the shells landed close to the edge of our trench. Amir and I were in the trench near the tire store and got lower into it. We were terrified each time we heard a shell whistling and exploding near us. I heard our artillery responding, and unlike in the past, they gave the Chetniks a long, intensive barrage. I heard other explosions in the distance. All our artillery in Sarajevo was firing for a long time. Then we heard small arms fire in the distance.

Saba told us that our soldiers made a major offensive to break the siege of Sarajevo. They pushed the Chetniks back in some places and briefly reached the outskirts of Pale. In our sector, the Chetniks continued to shell us, and we responded.

During a lull in the firing, Amir and I felt bored and decided to walk along the trench. We arrived at the part of the stream that was closest to our trench where we sometimes saw ducks. Recently, we had seen a duck there with her young and hoped they would appear again. We waited but didn't see them. Time passed without the ducks showing themselves. We felt bored and walked toward the front of the tire store.

Suddenly, strong automatic fire from the Chetniks was directed at the two of us. We got lower into the trench. The bullets were coming from the direction of Lipa, which was a higher location. They came into the trench and hit the wall and floor, showering us with dirt. We squeezed ourselves into the other side of the trench. I heard bullets whining around us. We expected them to stop firing, but instead more machine gun fire was shot at us. We couldn't move. They kept shooting. Each minute seemed like an hour. We thought they would never stop. Some of the bullets landed near us. Amir looked terrified.

He thought he would be hit by one of the bullets. Amir looked around, perhaps thinking about trying to run. I was afraid he would panic and lose control. So I held him down.

"Stay down!" I yelled. "Don't move!"

The machine guns kept shooting without a pause. It seemed that while one machine gunner stopped to reload his weapon, another kept firing. I was angry that our fellow soldiers didn't shoot at those machine gunners. But I knew they had orders to only shoot if they had a clear target. Finally, the gunfire stopped, and we slowly moved to a safer place.

We were shaking and afraid to leave the trench. Eventually, we went to Titova Vila.

I felt a terrible pain again in my chest in the trench, and it got worse at Titova Vila. I didn't talk to anybody about it, but Saba noticed me holding my chest and breathing heavily. He said I should see a doctor immediately.

"I already spoke to the doctor about this," I said. "He'll say the same thing to me."

"Perhaps he will, but when a soldier's sick, the commanding officer must send him to the doctor. I could get into trouble for ignoring you."

The doctor read my medical history and examined me. He wrote something down on a form and said he was giving me extra time to stay at home. When I brought the note to Saba, he allowed me to take days off and say goodbye to Amir.

At the flat, I felt depressed. It seemed like my heart problems would never end. My mother and sister tried to cheer me up, but I didn't feel like talking.

On July 7 at around 2 p.m., somebody knocked at the door, and I opened it. It was Ismet Nokto, my cousin, and he was carrying Amir's boots under his arm. Even though he didn't say a word, my mother and I both knew something terrible happened. The boots told us more than Ismet's expression. They had blood spots on them.

My mother's eyes opened wide, and her cheeks shook. She said slowly, "Is my son…"

"No, Amir was wounded in the leg but not too seriously," he interrupted in a calm, quiet voice. "He's in the hospital at this moment."

My mother didn't believe him. Her eyes asked many questions, but she was too upset to put them into words. She trembled, and her voice was shaking. Ismet said my father was with Amir and gave him the boots.

I also didn't believe Ismet because of past bad experiences with him. In 1993, I saw Ismet give a can of fish to his cat. I kept silent but couldn't understand how he could feed his animal while people in Sarajevo were starving. I was angry at him. Later, Ismet was in charge of medical supplies and medical directives, a very important position. Even though doctors declared some soldiers unfit to return to the front, Ismet overruled those orders and sent them to the trenches anyway. Many people hated Ismet and cursed him because of that. Ismet never went to medical school but considered himself higher than a doctor. It was also very difficult to talk to Ismet.

My mother sent me to the hospital to see if Amir was seriously wounded or not. As I walked there, I felt terrible. I had promised to cover my brother's back, but when the time came to help him, I wasn't there.

I wondered how my father and Ismet knew about Amir's wound. They were at different fronts. I thought because Ismet was in charge of medical directives, he had seen a report about Amir being wounded. I was wrong. I heard later that Ismet was visiting Stojcevac when Amir was wounded, and he told my father.

The hospital was a former department store. Its outside

was full of shrapnel and bullet holes, but it was recently built, just before the war, and in good condition. When I entered, I was told the basement was used as a first aid station. There was no heating, and the basement was very damp. There were many wounded soldiers placed close together in a small area, and their beds were made of boards. Some were crying in pain. Someone directed me to the back of the building where I saw my father in front of a closed door.

"Where's Amir?" I asked him.

"They just gave him first aid."

"How is he?"

"He was wounded in the leg but not badly."

"I'd like to see him."

"The surgeon will not let you in."

"Why? Did they operate on Amir?"

"No, they didn't operate yet. They cleaned the wound and bandaged it."

I was angry he wouldn't let me visit my brother, but this wasn't the place or the time to argue. I ran back to my mother and told her what my father said. She still didn't believe Amir wasn't wounded badly. Her chin kept shaking. That day, she couldn't stop sighing and crying. Jasmina kept holding her.

That night, Amir came home on crutches with my father. He was in great pain. The surgeon didn't want to remove the shrapnel from his right leg. He hoped it would come out by itself.

Amir told me what happened in the trench. A shell hit a tree and exploded high above him. Shrapnel rained down on him and other soldiers, but only he was wounded. Mujo (the Gypsy) just received a scratch.

Amir mostly lay on his bed. We brought him food and cleaned his wound. It was constantly filled with pus. He went to the doctor regularly.

"The surgeon was afraid if he tried to remove the shrapnel, there would be too much damage, and he might have to amputate the leg," Amir said to me. "That's why he hoped it would come out on its own. But it's not coming out. They'll have to operate."

"The wound doesn't look too bad," I said. "You shouldn't have trouble."

"The wound does look bad," he said. "I know many people who became invalids in this war. I have sympathy for them, but I don't want to be one of them. If I lose my leg, my life will be over. Nobody will hire me. No woman will be interested in me. I'll be limping around on crutches or sitting in a wheelchair for the rest of my life."

I spent most of the night sitting at Amir's bed. Much of the time, we spoke about the interesting times we spent together. Some of the time, I sat quietly thinking of another subject to talk about. I kept the conversation away from Amir's wound. Finally, Amir closed his eyes and went to sleep. I got into my bed and went to sleep with a prayer on my lips that the surgeon wouldn't remove his leg.

The next morning, my father and I took Amir back to the hospital. He was taken in for surgery. Since there was no waiting room, we sat on chairs at the entrance of the operating room. My father and I didn't talk. We just glanced at each other and at the door. Finally, the surgeon walked out of the door with a smile and looked at us. A feeling of relief came over me.

The shrapnel was removed successfully. It was four inches long. The surgeon said that Amir was lucky. If the shrapnel had taken a different route, it would have cut off his leg. He said he had had to do many amputations of people who were wounded with a smaller piece of shrapnel.

While Amir was recuperating, I went back to Stojcevac.

There, I heard that the Chetniks finally captured Srebrenica, a town northeast of Sarajevo near the Serbian border.

Srebrenica was a UN "safe area" and surrounded by Serbian troops since the war began. On July 11, 1995, the Chetniks finally overwhelmed the town's defenders and took control over the Srebrenica. Muslim men and women were separated. About 23,000 women were taken by buses to Muslim controlled territories, and the men were taken to warehouses and later killed. About 5,000 Muslims were at a UN base, seeking protection from the Serbs. UN troops surrendered those people in exchange for UN soldiers the Serbs held hostage. Most of those Muslims were also killed. About 15,000 Muslim soldiers escaped Srebrenica, but they were shelled, shot at, and captured as they attempted to go through the forest and mountains to Muslim controlled areas.

About 7,500 Muslims were murdered in Srebrenica, making it the worst crime of the war and largest mass killing in Europe since World War II. I didn't know anyone from Srebrenica but felt bad for the people there.

Two weeks later, the Chetniks conquered the town of Zepa, which was also a UN "safe area" and surrounded by Serbian troops. Like Srebrenica, it was also "ethnically cleansed."

Another cease-fire was declared. After a heavy rain, Ramiz and I came out of the trench because it was full of water, and there were many mosquitos in it. There were sporadic outbursts of gunfire at night, but during the day, it was quiet. About 32 yards behind us, we saw a woman with a cow.

"She shouldn't be so close to the front line," I said. "She might get shot. I'll tell her to go away."

"Don't go! I'll warn her she's not allowed to be here," Ramiz said as he ran to her.

I expected him to come back soon, but he wanted to stay

169

there and talk to the woman. He was lonely and missed his wife. I felt sorry for him and decided not to bother them. The time went by slowly, and Ramiz didn't return. He enjoyed the woman's company and forgot what he was asked to do.

I heard bullets fly past me and jumped into the trench, feeling frightened and confused because it seemed unbelievable I wasn't shot.

"Elvir," a voice that sounded like Ramiz called out. I thought he was wounded.

"Are you okay?" I called out.

"Come here," he called out.

I crawled to the place where they were. I saw Ramiz crouching beside the woman who was laying on her back, unconscious, and bleeding very badly. She was thin, around 35, had brown hair, and was wearing traditional clothes Bosnian Muslim village women wear called a dimijie.

"What should I do?" Ramiz asked, looking at me with his eyes wide and full of tears. His face was covered with sweat.

"Go to the sergeant, and tell him to call an ambulance and bring bandages and a stretcher immediately! Hurry up!" Ramiz ran off.

I examined the woman. Blood started pouring from her mouth in enormous amounts. I turned her over. A dumdum bullet had hit her in her back and exploded in her lung causing severe injuries. She didn't have a chance of staying alive, but in spite of that, I continued to bandage her wound. When she died, I turned her on her back.

A minute later, while I was still leaning above her, her body jerked as if she wanted to sit in order to kiss me on the cheek. Instead, blood poured from her mouth and covered my clothes.

The next day, Ramiz just stood in the trench without talking, and I didn't try to begin a conversation. Finally he spoke, "I only think about myself. I should have told that woman to leave the front line. If I was thinking about her instead of myself, she'd still be alive." He burst into tears.

Ramiz kept crying for hours, and I tried to comfort him. I told him it was that woman's destiny to die, and he couldn't change a person's destiny. But he kept on crying. I was upset as well and blamed myself for the woman's death, but I didn't want to show it.

When I went home on leave, it was a relief. My mother had a worried look on her face.

"Your father was wounded in the head in the battle for Vidovac," she said. (Vidovac was a hill between Mount Igman and Mount Trebevic, a mountain in the southeast of Sarajevo.)

"Tell me more about it."

"He came home and told me what happened. Because they had so many injured in the hospital, they couldn't keep him there. After he was home for five or six hours, he said he felt dizzy and fainted. The blood drained from his face, and his face turned white. Our neighbor Rasim took him to the hospital, and he's been there for ten days. The doctor said he had a concussion."

My father was in the same hospital where Amir had stayed. I again saw wounded soldiers crying on boards. I felt sad that my father was wounded but not too sad. I visited him because I had to. I considered it an obligation. He was lying on a board with a bandage on his head. He opened his eyes, and we had the shortest conversation.

"How do you feel?" I asked.

"Dizzy. I have pain in my head."

I shrugged my shoulders and kept quiet for a minute.

"I have to go," I said and left.

I thought maybe because he was wounded and his life was

in danger, he might apologize for the way he had treated me and the family. He didn't apologize, and even if he had, I wasn't sure I could forgive him because it was impossible to forget the suffering he had put me through.

Amir didn't heal completely. His leg was still swollen and caused him pain. However, the time Amir was allowed off the front line had passed, and we had to return to Stojcevac. Meho, Gula, and Ramiz cheered when they saw Amir, and Gula poked him on his nose.

At Titova Vila, Amir told me about a conversation he'd just had with Saba. "Saba told me that our forces are expected to fight a new battle around Sarajevo, and they need every able bodied man. They ordered me to be part of the unit that will fight in the battle."

"Forget it. The commission ordered you to be with me in the invalid unit."

"Saba said the commission specifically ordered me to be part of this new operation and said when the battle was over, I could return to this unit."

"The commission is getting revenge for forcing them to change their decision. I'll talk to Mido Botulja again to stop that."

"No, I want to be part of the force to finally end the Chetnik siege."

"Do you want to be killed?"

"No, I'm going and will return after the battle. You can't protect me always, Elvir. We both discovered that recently."

"Amir, you just got over a wound that isn't completely healed," I said. "The battle will be won or lost without you. Let's talk to Saba and find a way to keep you here."

But Amir was determined to take part in the battle and wouldn't listen to me.

"Be careful and good luck," I finally said. Soon, he left.

In the beginning of August, Croatian forces launched Operation Storm against the Krajina region of Croatia. Two days into the attack, Knin, the capital of the Krajina fell. By the end of the attack, the remaining areas of the Krajina, except for eastern Slavonia, fell to the Croatians. There were thousands of Serbian refugees from the Krajina.

At the same time, our forces began an offensive, and we heard explosions from our artillery. Our objective was to try to cut the ring around Sarajevo and connect Gorazde with Sarajevo. Our forces approached a town south of Sarajevo called Trnovo, located west of Gorazde. People in Gorazde could hear the explosions of our weapons and were expecting to be freed by Corpus I (the First Corps), the army unit in charge of that battle. Our forces didn't enter Gorazde, but we ended the siege of it. It was during this battle that the person in command of Corpus I, General Immanovic was killed. We heard about his heroics and were upset about his death.

At the end of August, two Serbian shells landed in a central market in Sarajevo, killing 37 people and wounding 80. Like the attack last year at the "Markale," bodies, pieces of bodies, and blood were all over the sidewalk. In response, NATO began a massive bombing campaign of Serb controlled areas.

Our forces began another offensive to the north and conquered more territory occupied by the Serbs. Our forces advanced fast, and we expected Banja Luka, the capital of the Srpska Republic to fall.

I returned home and saw pictures of this battle on TV. General Atif Dudakovic stayed in front with his army. I saw him take off his boots, walk into a river and give orders to the soldiers, "Go ahead. Go ahead. Don't stop." The Chetniks retreated in panic. They left their tanks and heavy artillery behind. The

Bosnian army also attacked Serbian positions in Croatia from where they were sending missiles and shells at us.

We had already conquered 21 percent more of Bosnia and were about to capture Banja Luka. Then we heard the UN state that if Banja Luka was defeated, there would be a human catastrophe because of the Serbian refugees. NATO threatened to bomb our army if we continued, so we stopped. We were not happy about this.

The soldiers agreed that most of the refugees from the war came from Serbian controlled areas where they "ethnically cleansed" the non-Serb population. Since our troops didn't and wouldn't "ethnically cleanse" the Serbs, there wouldn't be refugees.

We also didn't understand why our government was concerned about NATO threats to bomb us. They threatened the Chetniks for years before they bombed them.

Amir finally returned to Stojcevac in good health and with stories. The Chetniks sent a storm of shell fire at his unit, and many soldiers were killed. When our soldiers conquered their trenches, the Chetniks put up some resistance and fled. Amir also heard about members of the mujahedeen who joined us in the battle and men from China, Romania, and Bulgaria who fought with the Chetniks in Trnovo.

The mujahedeen were fundamentalist Islamic warriors from Muslim countries such as Iran, Turkey, Afghanistan, Pakistan, and Saudi Arabia. They first fought against the Soviet occupation troops in Afghanistan in the 1980s and later with Muslim troops in wars in Bosnia, Chechnya, Kosovo, Somalia, and other places.

After the battle, Amir was assigned to carry the dead off the battlefield. He found it unbelievable to carry dead people who just a few hours before were in good health and he had had conversations with.

Amir and I were in the trench near the tire store when intensive artillery shelling began near our position. Finally the shelling subsided, and it became quiet. There was sporadic firing from both sides. We heard people talking. Soon, we heard more shooting and after that, silence. Then we heard someone calling for help. We ran down the trench toward the sound and saw a soldier who was wounded in his leg near his testicles. He was bleeding and crying from the pain. I didn't know his name because he had recently joined our unit. The trench was narrow, and there wasn't enough room to give him first aid.

"There isn't enough room to help you here, so we'll have to take you to better place," I said to him. He nodded.

We dragged him sideways through the trench and tried to be gentle, but he kept yelling in pain. I called out to other people to help us, but nobody answered. We kept moving him, and I saw a line of blood spots along the trench. He continued to scream.

Finally, we stopped at a wider area. Saba came with the medic Izo and other soldiers. They stopped his bleeding, cleaned him up, and tried to bandage the wound. But it was difficult to cover this particular area with bandages. The bandages didn't do much good.

Other soldiers came, and they took the wounded soldier away. They carried him behind a hill so they wouldn't be shot. This was the last war casualty I saw.

CHAPTER ELEVEN

THE WAR ENDS

On October 12, 1995, a cease-fire was negotiated, and both sides agreed to begin peace talks. Hours before the cease-fire began, the Serbs began a massive "ethnic cleansing" campaign in Banja Luka.

Two weeks after the cease-fire, the Bosnian Serbs began freeing male Muslim civilians in exchange for Serbian prisoners of war.

In the beginning of November, peace talks began at the Wright-Patterson Air Force Base, near Dayton, Ohio. President Clinton met with the presidents of Croatia, Bosnia, and Serbia. It was agreed to split Bosnia into two separate states. The Muslim-Croatian Federation would get 51 percent of Bosnia, and the Srpska Republic would consist of 49 percent of Bosnia. This plan was proposed by the UN in 1994 and got support from Milosevic. However, it had been rejected then by Karadzic because his troops controlled 70 percent of Bosnia. Now that his troops had lost territory and were bombed regularly by NATO, he agreed to the division.

There would be a jagged border between Bosnia and the Srpska Republic. Bosnia or the Muslim-Croatian Federation would consist of territories on the west and center of the country, including the cities and towns of Sarajevo, Bihac, Tuzla, Gorazde, Ilidza, Hrasnica, and Mostar. The Republic of Srpska would include the cities and towns of Pale, Foca, Zepa, Srebrenica, Banja Luka, Visegrad, and Prijedor. The Republic of Srpska border would run on the outskirts of the south of Sarajevo with a southern portion of Dobrinja belonging to them.

The soldiers in my unit didn't like Bosnia being split into two separate states. Most of them loudly cursed the people who made that agreement possible. We bristled at the unfairness. Rewarding the hateful Serbs was a bitter pill for us to swallow.

Part of the agreement called for the presence of 60,000 NATO troops called the Implementation/Stabilization Force (including 20,000 Americans) to keep the warring parties from launching further attacks. Those troops would be able to remove troops or weapons from any location and could use force to accomplish that removal. Unlike the UN troops, these troops had the armor and weapons to carry out their mission.

Part of the agreement said that refugees could return to their homes and have their property returned to them. However, many Muslim homes were destroyed.

Another part of the agreement said that people indicted for war crimes should be turned over to the international War Crimes Tribunal in The Hague. NATO troops could bring those people into custody.

The most notable people indicted by the tribunal were Radovan Karadzic and Ratko Mladic, but they evaded arrest, and the Serbian and Bosnian Serb authorities have not surrendered them as of this writing.

Another part of the agreement declared that eastern Slavonia, the part of the Krajina not recaptured by Croatian troops, would be peacefully returned to Croatia. One of the cities in eastern Slavonia was Vukovar, which had suffered so much during the 1991 war.

All soldiers were obligated to move away from the front line. However, neither side trusted the other, and some soldiers stayed. Both sides removed all their weapons except for some automatic guns. After the peace treaty was signed, only five or six soldiers with automatics stayed in the trenches and were ordered to constantly walk along them. Also, the time we stayed at Stojcevac was reduced. I kept guard in the trench for two days and went home for six days.

Because of this, we went home more often for a longer time. Amir and my father recovered fully from their wounds, and the food situation improved. No longer would we have to go over the mountain to Pazaric to get food. The sound of shooting and shelling stopped. After three and a half years, I was accustomed to that sound, and the silence made me feel uneasy. Also, electricity, telephone service, and water service were finally restored to Hrasnica and most of Sarajevo.

Our commander Saba surprised Amir and me by inviting us to his flat in Hrasnica to meet his fiancee. During the war, Saba was friendly but polite and reserved, and I felt it would be interesting to see him relaxed in his flat instead of giving orders on the front. When we got there, I was surprised to discover that his fiancee was Edisa Muzur, a friend from school. Edisa and I told each other about our experiences during the war and the friends we lost.

Like other people, Saba didn't like the peace agreement. "Bosnia was once a strong country," he said. "Now it's two weak countries. Bosnia is being divided according to ethnic and religious lines. What's that all about? How dare the UN reward the murderers of thousands of civilians with their own state? Our government should have ordered us to continue our attack whatever the UN or NATO said."

"What are your future plans?" I asked him.

"I lived in Foca before the war, but I can't go back there. Foca will be part of the Srpska Republic, and the Serbs will not welcome me back. I'll stay in the army and live here."

In Bosnia, most of the Serbian houses weren't touched. In the Srpska Republic, every Muslim mosque was destroyed, along with many Muslim homes. With the end of the war, we expected the Serbs to act the same. The Muslims I knew were fearful to go to areas controlled by the Serbs.

Meho also invited Amir and me to his home to meet his wife. After we introduced ourselves, we sat in his dining room and talked. Meho's wife poured each of us a cup of coffee. As I sipped it, I realized it was good coffee, not ersatz coffee.

"This tastes like real coffee," I said.

"It is real coffee," Meho said with a smile.

"I thought real coffee was only available to high officers," I said.

"It is," Meho said. "But being the former owner of a large bakery and having lots of money has its advantages."

In the trench, Meho constantly said how jealous he was of his wife, and every time she went out, even to visit her parents, he went into a tirade and refused to believe her. He was sure she was dating other men. Worrying about his wife's activities became an obsession for him. However, now that we met her, Meho's wife seemed to be a decent, honest person, and my opinion was that his suspicions were baseless. She also seemed patient and understanding, and Meho would need someone like that to help him with his psychological problems resulting from his detention camp experiences.

Ramiz was finally able to visit his wife in Croatia. When he returned to Stojcevac, the sour look on his face told me he had bad news about her.

"My wife refused to return with me to Bosnia," he said. "When I asked her why, she said what I was worried about. She and her boss are seeing each other romantically. They don't live together now, but that will change soon. She wants to divorce me and get custody of the children."

I kept silent. I couldn't think of anything to say, but I did feel sorry for him.

Ramiz told me his wife suggested he could move to Croatia, but he refused. He complained about his wife's boss taking advantage of his absence and of his wife betraying him.

"We've been through so much together, good times and bad," he said. "How could she hurt me?"

Ramiz cried for hours, and I tried to comfort him.

In December 1995, NATO troops set up positions in Bosnia. I saw tanks, armored vehicles, and heavily armed troops all over Stojcevac. If only we had this force during the war! NATO troops cleared the land mines between the trenches, and their tanks rode between the trenches next to the stream. Our soldiers with uniforms were ordered to wear civilian clothes. When NATO troops came to our trench looking for weapons, we were told to hide them.

When the first tanks came near us, we hid our weapons and waited. Heavily armed, helmeted NATO soldiers jumped off their tanks, glanced at us and walked through our trench looking around. They were French and English troops. I could understand some of what the English soldiers were saying but was too shy to speak to them. They didn't have interpreters and didn't try to talk to us. They walked back to their tanks without finding our weapons and rode away. Later, NATO troops kept walking back and forth between the trenches.

My heart was giving me problems again at the front line,

and it got worse at home. My mother and father noticed me breathing heavily and said I should tell Saba and go to the hospital.

"I've been to the hospital," I said. "They said they didn't have the facilities to help me, and I should come back after the war."

"The war is over," my mother said.

"I'm still on the front line."

"The fighting has stopped," she said. "Go to the hospital."

"Mother, when..." I began.

"Listen to your mother," my father interrupted.

Saba gave me a pass to see the doctor in Hrasnica, and I again went to Kosevo Hospital. Because of an agreement with the Serbs, I was able to take a bus across the airport. More trams and buses took me most of the way.

Because of the end of the fighting, Kosevo Hospital had fewer patients and less waiting time. While a nurse was giving me an EKG, I had another attack and could hardly breathe. The nurse had her back to me. She looked at the paper and saw the line flatten. She yelled for a doctor. One came into the room, and he looked at the paper too. The attack finally passed, and the pain ended.

"How do you feel?" the doctor asked me.

"I feel well."

The doctor glanced at the EKG machine and looked back at me. "You must stay at the hospital for at least a week starting now. We'll have to give you more tests."

"Please delay that. I have to inform my parents. My mother would worry if I don't show up. I also have to inform my army unit."

"I'll give you two days. I'll write a note to your commander to give you a medical leave."

After those days, I returned and was admitted to a wing of the hospital called The Third Internal Clinic For Heart Illnesses. They kept giving me injections in my arm, medicines to drink, and took more EHO scans.

"Why do I have to stay in the hospital?" I asked the doctor.

"You have some kind of a block," he said.

I didn't understand. "What kind of a block?"

"It's the same thing as a heart attack but doesn't make you unconscious. It's an easier attack. However, I'm afraid of complications. Because of that, I recommend that you stay in the hospital for a while."

I was put into a large room with 10 patients. Most were older men in their sixties and seventies. I was the youngest and felt uncomfortable. The patients spoke only about their illnesses and heart problems.

One of the patients claimed he had been clinically dead for a few minutes, and the doctors revived him. I decided to question him.

"What was that like?" I asked. I thought he would say that he saw a bright light or angels, but he surprised me.

"I remember everything before I went into a coma and lost consciousness. I felt chest pain and thought I was dying. I remember in the ambulance, the doctors were loud while giving me first aid. Then I lost consciousness and nothing. When I woke up, the doctor said I died for a few minutes."

I read books about people who were clinically dead and revived. They saw angels, lights, diseased family members, felt a glow of love, and were high above in the sky. I expected to hear something like that and was upset that I didn't. Could it be that after you die, there is nothing?

I felt bad, and after listening to that man, I felt worse. Feeling depressed, I kept quiet and only spoke when someone asked me something.

Smoking wasn't allowed in the hospital, but the craving for

a cigarette was driving me crazy. I felt nervous and unhappy all day and wanted to run away. I couldn't bear it.

I went into the hall, looking to see where other people went to smoke. I saw some people go into the bathroom and stay there for a while. I concluded they must be smoking in there. After hesitating, I decided to go in.

The door wasn't shut fully, and when I entered, I saw a woman of about 45 and a man over 60. They were sitting on a bench in the back of the bathroom and moved very fast when I walked in, as though they were surprised. They thought I was a staff person, but after looking at me, realized I wasn't.

"Dedo (grandfather), whenever we want to do something, someone interrupts us," the woman said to the man.

The man tried to straighten out the wrinkles in the woman's coat and apron. I felt embarrassed. Maybe, they wanted to make love, and I had interrupted them. I wanted to leave but just stared at them. Finally, I told them I came here to smoke.

"Then smoke," the man said. "Just close the door fully and lock it."

I did that, and the cigarette relaxed me.

"I'm Angelina. What's your name?" the woman asked, and I told her.

"I like my meat well done, but I like it rare too," she said to me. "You're a good looking guy and well built, Elvir. What do you think about making love with older women?"

I felt embarrassed. She then told vulgar jokes, and I felt shy and kept quiet.

A few days later, Angelina and I became friends and talked in an informal way. The vulgar jokes stopped.

It was the custom for the older patients to play jokes on the newer patient, and they decided to play a joke on me. After midnight, patients went into the doctors' lounge to smoke and drink coffee. The doctors didn't use it then. One time, they invited me there, and when I entered, they treated me like a king. They bowed before me, and someone said, "Announcing, Elvir Kulin." The room was crowded, but someone got up and let me sit in his chair. As I sat and talked, a woman five or six years older than me came into the room, greeted us, and looked around for a seat.

"There's no place for me to sit," she said. She hesitated for a while and approached me.

"Never mind, here's a good place to sit," she said and sat on my lap. She didn't sit with her back to me but straddled her legs around my waist and faced me. I felt very uncomfortable. My face was near her breasts. When I turned my head, she moved, and put her breasts near my face again. The other patients stared at us and smiled.

Seven or eight days after I arrived at the hospital, a new patient came, and the patients embarrassed him as well. We got into a large column of people, one behind another at his bed. Each person shook hands with him and introduced himself or herself. In Bosnia, when you introduce yourself to a new person, the custom is to say your full name. Just saying "Hello." is considered rude. Therefore, this new man had to repeat his name to each person and looked confused and embarrassed. His cheeks were red and blazing with self-consciousness and impatience. Angelina was in front of me. After she introduced herself, she turned to me and said, "This is Elvir, and he is my husband." I felt embarrassed but didn't correct her. "It's nice to meet you," I said to the man. I didn't think he believed her, and I forgot about it.

Later, that man came into my room carrying a chess set, and he walked up to me.

"Do you want to play chess with me?" he asked.

"I really don't know how to play chess well."

He insisted, and I gave in.

As we moved our first pieces, he asked, "What's it like to be with a woman who's old enough to be your mother?"

I was confused. "What woman?" Then I remembered what Angelina said and laughed. He believed her.

"People like to joke around here," I said.

"I guess harmless joking doesn't hurt anyone," he said. "After what we were through, we could use a few laughs."

I barely knew how to play chess, and the man beat me easily.

In the next bed, there was a man named Zoka, and he was mentally retarded. He was born in 1964 but acted like a child of three or four. He kept getting up at night and urinating into the sink. A few times, I let it go and pretended I didn't hear anything, but eventually I couldn't stand it anymore.

"Zoka, what are you doing?" I asked the next time I heard him doing it.

"Nothing," he responded and went back to his bed.

"We have a bathroom for that."

However, Zoka kept peeing in the sink. I was going crazy, and it was difficult dealing with him.

Zoka stayed up at night and talked to himself. He kept saying over and over, "My sister is coming today to visit me. Will my sister come?" until the morning. He spent most of his time looking out the window, waiting for her. He was very devoted.

It was sad to see him disappointed during visiting hours when his sister didn't come. He kept silent for a long time and sat on his bed looking at something in front of him as though he was looking through the wall. I felt sorry for him.

Zoka had severe edema in his body, and his legs were swollen. His testicles were blown up like a male sheep. He suffered a great deal and couldn't sleep at night. He kept saying to himself, "Mother, it's terrible. I can't stand this."

Whenever Zoka complained, I left the room and called the

doctor to help him. They injected him so much that his arms were covered with bruises. When the doctors came, Zoka pretended everything was okay, but his legs were so swollen that he could hardly move.

I wanted to visit my flat for a weekend, but the doctor wanted me to stay. "You're not well. I can't risk my job because of you. It would be better if you stayed in the hospital," he said.

However, I had to get a decent meal and a shower, so I decided to go. I was afraid that Zoka would say something to the doctor about my leaving, so I promised him chocolate cakes when I got back. He loved sweets.

When I returned to the hospital, there were policemen around the building with dogs and security people everywhere. At the entrance, I was stopped by a policeman.

"Who are you?" he asked me. "Where do you want to go?"

"I'm a patient here."

"How could a young, healthy guy be a patient in a hospital? I don't believe it."

"I have a heart condition." I told him my name.

"I'll have to check the list of patients with the receptionist. Stand over there," he pointed as he went into the hospital. I stood to the side with men in white, perhaps doctors.

A large car stopped in front of us, and several men wearing suits and ties jumped out. One of them was a man in his fifties, and I recognized him from TV. It was Bosnian Vice President Ejup Ganic. A doctor recognized Ganic too and said his name. Ganic heard his name mentioned, shook hands and said, "How are you?" to each of us standing there, including me, and went into the hospital with the other men.

The policeman returned. He had found my name on the list and let me through. When I got to my room, I was told the reason for the police, the security guards, and Ganic's appearance.

Izetbegovic had had a heart attack and was in intensive care in this hospital.

I then remembered the night before I left, I saw an ambulance arrive in front of the building. That must have been Izetbegovic.

Finally, the doctors confirmed the diagnosis of an Atrial Septal Defect that was already stated in my medical documentation. They noticed there was another abnormality in my heart, but couldn't see it with the EHO, and I should have a TEE scan. Because of the lack of equipment, that scan was impossible now. I should come back in five years.

"What should I do now?" I asked a doctor.

"You had problems when the war started because of a poor diet, stress, and climbing up mountains. Now, you should eat better, have more balanced foods, try to reduce your stress, and only walk on level ground. Your attacks should subside. Also, you should stop smoking."

"It's very difficult to stop smoking. I'm addicted."

"Which is more difficult, to stop smoking or to be sick all the time? How important is your life?"

After 18 days, I left the hospital, returned home and went to the trench. NATO troops were still inspecting our trench and looking for weapons. My family and fellow soldiers hoped for good news about my medical condition. Unfortunately, I had none.

I heard that NATO troops were paying Muslims and Serbians to build latrines, construct encampments, bake bread, cut hair, move trash, and clean clothes for them. Because I knew English, I decided to apply for a job as an English interpreter and translator with them.

There was a large British NATO encampment in Hrasnica, and I applied for a job there. I thought that NATO soldiers would be happy to hear a Bosnian speaking English. But they just glanced at me. I filled out an application. A British officer asked me a few questions and said if they needed me, they would call. While there, I noticed the other English translators and interpreters were all young, attractive Bosnian women. I wasn't surprised the British didn't call me. I was the wrong sex.

In the new year, 1996, Serbian and Bosnian troops pulled back from their positions to areas in their states. With them, came the civilians, mostly Serbian. Muslim civilians in the Srpska Republic were already "ethnically cleansed." In Ilidza, Grbavica, Lukavica, and the hills around Sarajevo, Serbians packed their belongings into trucks, cars, and wagons and left for the Srpska Republic. Karadzic told them they would be in danger if they stayed.

Before leaving, Serbs burned down buildings and houses in Ilidza and Grbavica. We saw smoke from the fires. The Serbs seemed to be saying if they had to leave their homes, Muslims wouldn't be moving into them. NATO troops and Muslim firemen under NATO protection had to put out the fires and rescue people because the Serbian fire department refused to do the job. How could they be so cruel?

I didn't understand the Serbs' hatred of us. Unlike Muslims living in Serbian-controlled areas, I didn't hear about Serbs in Hrasnica being harmed. An example was Milka Krvavac, our Serbian neighbor. She and her daughter were never touched by Muslims in Hrasnica during the war. After the war, I heard that Milka got back together with her ex-husband who was a Chetnik. They and their daughter moved to Rogatica in the Srpska Republic and then to Serbia.

Saba invited me into his office in Stojcevac. "Headquarters ordered me to ask the soldiers if they want to sign a contract to stay in the Bosnian army for a few more years," he said. "You'll get regular pay, food, lodgings, and a uniform. What do you say, Elvir?"

I laughed. "I was in the army during the war for three years and didn't get a uniform. Now, that the war is over, I'll get one. That's very funny. I must refuse to sign that contract."

"I'll make a career in the army. Sometimes, the army is the way to go."

The army was indeed the way to go for Croatian President Franjo Tudjman. He joined the partisans during World War II, became a major general in the Yugoslavian National Army in 1960, and was elected president of Croatia in 1990. But I didn't think I could attain the position of major general or president of a country if I stayed in the army. Also, army life didn't appeal to me.

"The army is not the way for me," I said. "I had enough of it."

Saba laughed. "I understand." He took out a form. "I have good news for you. The government will be giving veteran's certificates for all discharged soldiers who served honorably in the Bosnian army that can be used for money, to buy land, to start a business, or to go to college. Just fill out this form, and you'll receive your document." He put the form on the desk, and I filled it out.

I heard that Saba asked Amir, Gula, Ramiz, and Meho to sign the contract, and they all refused. They filled out the forms to get their certificates.

In March 1996, the last day on the front arrived, and we got our discharge papers. At Titova Vila, the soldiers who were still there had a party. I considered many of them to be my family and would miss them. We all felt uneasy about the future of living in a destroyed and divided country.

We each spoke about what we would do after the war; many

people didn't know. Most of their former places of employment were destroyed or badly damaged, including the textile store Ramiz worked at and Meho's bakery.

We wished each other good luck. We would need it.

Epilogue

LIFE AFTER THE WAR

Sarajevo became a city (and Hrasnica a settlement) full of destroyed buildings, shell holes, disabled people in wheelchairs, and armed NATO troops patrolling the streets. It looked like a city in Germany immediately after World War II. Between Ilidza and Hrasnica and Ilidza and Sarajevo was a huge minefield, and I saw yellow tape around the area.

Out of a 4.4 million pre-war population, about 278,000 people were killed in Bosnia. Most were Bosnian Muslims. I lost friends and relatives. I was lucky. Fortunately, nobody in my immediate family was killed, and I wasn't wounded.

There were around two million refugees at the end of the war. About 800,000 of them left the country. The rest were internally displaced throughout Bosnia. Slowly, refugees began to return.

Between 600,000 to one million land mines were scattered throughout Bosnia. Only 60 percent of the minefields were identified. Yellow tape marked many of those minefields.

My sister's grocery store was in Alipasino polje, which was under our control during the war and behind the front lines. However, many buildings and houses near our store were destroyed or damaged by shells. It was the same situation with our store. It had shell holes and was badly damaged. When Jasmina abandoned the store in 1992, she left some food behind, thinking the war would end soon, and she would be going back. As we walked into the store, more damage and empty shelves greeted us.

We begged and borrowed money from relatives and friends and finally had the damage repaired. Croatia had food all through the war, and we got food from the suppliers there. Money for food was a problem, and we had to borrow it from relatives too. We promised to repay them as soon as customers came in to make their purchases.

Before the war, Jasmina and her husband Osama co-owned the store. Now, with Osama's disappearance, Jasmina changed the ownership documents so that she was the store's sole owner.

Amir, Jasmina, and I worked hard to make the store a success. Some of our first customers were NATO troops. They were from different countries, and we heard different languages: French, British, Dutch, Italian, and others. Most of them didn't seem friendly and didn't talk to us. They just put their food on the counter and paid for it. Their attitudes might have been because they didn't know where our sympathies lay. Slowly, we began to make a profit and pay back some of the money people had lent us.

The war had interrupted my last year of school, and I wasn't able to finish. After the war, I went back, graduated, and was ready to go to the university.

Located near the National and University Library, the Sarajevo University had departments in agriculture, forestry, medicine, law, teacher training, engineering, philosophy, and economics. Although the university continued to function during the war, there were fewer employees and students, mostly because they were mobilized into the army. Some buildings and equipment were damaged or destroyed by Serbian shells. Also, hundreds of refugees were housed in dormitories and other buildings during the war.

Armed with my veteran's certificate, I showed up at the Sarajevo University, ready to pursue my dream to get a degree to become an English teacher. My dream soon became a nightmare. I was directed to an administrator who said my certificate was worthless.

"It can't be worthless!" I argued. "At the end of the war, my commanding officer said honorably discharged soldiers could exchange this document for money, to buy land, to start a business, or to go to college."

"Things have changed since the end of the war," he said sadly.

He said to get money to rebuild Bosnia, our government got loans from the International Monetary Fund and the World Bank. One of the conditions for those loans was that state properties be privatized. The money allocated to the veteran certificates was transferred to privatization agencies.

The word "privatization" was heard all over Bosnia and all over the world. All countries that borrowed money from the fund had to change former state enterprises into private properties.

In Bosnia, the privatization process was in full swing. Many factories were privatized. Many businesses were put into private hands. The telephone companies became partly owned by a private company. The electric company wasn't private yet, but we expected it to be soon.

My dream to become an English teacher was slipping away. The cost for a semester at the university here was $1,500. I didn't have that much money. The administrator said loans or grants would not be given to students now.

"For three years, I was on the front line under constant gunfire and shell fire," I said. "I risked my life to keep the Chetniks from surrounding and capturing Sarajevo. Is this how my government thanks me?"

"There is nothing I can do," he said.

The administrator suggested I wait. He said perhaps as the economy improved, the government would transfer money back to the certificates.

As I walked back home from the university, I felt terrible. I had never felt this bad before. I didn't like Tito, but at least under his rule, most education was free. It was his highest priority. It was the lowest priority of the International Monetary Fund and the World Bank.

Later, I heard that the government offered to buy back veteran's certificates for a fraction of their value, but I refused and decided to wait.

In the meantime, I went to English continuing education classes held in a public school. They charged less. The teacher in the first level was a Bosnian, and the teachers in the next levels were native English speakers. Our first teacher was a Bosnian Jewish woman named Branka. She didn't talk about her experiences during this war but said that most of her family were killed by the Nazis during World War II.

I heard that most Bosnian Jews lived in Sarajevo. However, other than Branka, I didn't meet any of them. I just read about them.

Before our war in 1992, there were about 3,000 Jews living in Bosnia. About a third of them lived in Sarajevo. The American Jewish Joint Distribution Committee carried out land and air evacuations of most of the Sarajevian Jews, as well as some

Muslims and Christians. At our war's end, about 600 Jews were left in Sarajevo.

The next English teacher was a woman named Preny. Unlike my first English teacher in elementary school, Preny didn't say I was the best English student in class. But she did say my essays were the best and read them out loud. Preny said she had lived in an orphanage in Sri Lanka until an Australian couple adopted her, and she moved to Australia.

The last English teacher was a man named Terrence from New York. He said he had lived a wild life when younger and went to many parties. At one party, he got drunk, met a girl, and married her the same day. Soon they got divorced. Some of Terrence's remarks made us laugh. Like Preny, Terrence didn't understand Bosnian. When a student did poorly on a test, he or she sometimes cursed in Bosnian. Terrence repeated that Bosnian curse and asked us what that word meant. We laughed but didn't translate the curse. I got high grades on all the tests that Terrence gave, and he said my English was very good.

Out of 30 students who started the continuing education class, only 10 finished in all levels. I was one of them. Unfortunately, that didn't allow me to be an English teacher at a public school. I was told I needed a university degree to do that.

To my surprise, Jasmina's husband, Osama Shaghati, showed up in Sarajevo and spoke to Jasmina in private. At the flat, Jasmina told us that Osama apologized for what he did. She said he was scared of being killed in the war, and his girlfriend provided him security. He left his girlfriend and wanted to get back together with Jasmina and work at her store.

"You can't be serious about having anything to do with him after what he did to you," my mother said to her. "Divorce him, and never see him again."

My brother and I agreed.

But Jasmina wouldn't follow our advice. "Osama was a decent guy once, and I'll give him one more chance," she said.

Jasmina decided that Osama could work at the store at least temporarily. As for them getting back together, she said she would wait and see if his behavior improved. She didn't have enough money to rent another flat anyway. Osama said he was living in Sarajevo with friends.

At first, everything worked out fine. Osama worked hard and tried to be friendly to Amir and me. However, we kept noticing money was missing from the cash register. A little was missing each time, and we suspected Osama. He denied it.

A friend told us that Osama was cheating with a woman again. My sister confronted him, and they had an argument. Not long afterwards, Osama disappeared, taking all the cash from the register. Jasmina wouldn't let us call the police. She didn't want to see his face again.

Jasmina tried two times to divorce Osama, but he didn't show up in court. According to Bosnian law, when a husband or wife misses three court appearances, a divorce is granted.

When Osama didn't show up for the third court date, they became officially divorced. I hoped this time, we had seen the last of Osama, and so far, he hasn't returned.

A few years later, Jasmina told me she wanted to get married again. When I asked her what kind of a man she might be interested in, she said, "I don't want my future husband to be one of those people who thinks the more he has, the more he wants. The only thing I can offer him is my love and understanding, and I expect the same from him. He doesn't have to be attractive but honest and faithful."

A woman in the neighborhood told me that Gula Merdanovic had died of liver cancer earlier in the year. I felt sad. Gula was more than a fellow soldier. He was a friend, and his presence in the trench had made a difficult time easier. During his time with us, he never said he was sick, or acted like he was ill. It was typical of Gula not to complain. He was a decent man, and I would miss him.

In the beginning of winter 1997, a friend named Suad Vrazalica was called to serve in the army of Bosnia and Herzegovina. At the age of 18, every male citizen of Bosnia had to report to the draft board, and if he passed the physical examination, had to serve in the army for at least two years. Suad used to live near us in Hrasnica, and now was living in Gorazde. It's customary that two weeks after joining, soldiers had a ceremony where they swore allegiance to the country and swore to protect it from enemies. A relative named Jasmina, two friends named Mustafa and Sabina, and I were invited to that ceremony, and we decided to go there by car.

Since we were near his home, I spoke about seeing my cousin Suad Paleta while we were in the vicinity. (Suad Paleta was in the Sarajevian Police Academy barracks when the Yugoslavian army attacked it in 1992 and had stayed with us in the beginning of the war before he returned to Gorazde. Later, we heard he joined his family in Grebak, near Gorazde, served with the commandos, and survived the war.) However, the other people didn't want to make any extra stops. They just wanted us to stay in Gorazde for a short time and get out as soon as possible.

Part of the peace treaty was that Sarajevo and Gorazde be part of Bosnia. Gorazde was surrounded on three sides by territory belonging to the Srpska Republic, and there was a land corridor between Sarajevo and Gorazde. A road was built in the corridor, but it ran over mountains and hills and was difficult to get across. An easier way was to go through level roads between the mountains, but it ran through the Srpska Republic, and we hesitated. We didn't know how the Serbs would treat us. Finally, we decided to quickly drive through, and not stop or talk to anyone.

There weren't any border guards on the road between Bosnia and the Srpska Republic; there was just a sign that said: "You Are Entering The Sprska Republic." On the road, we saw other vehicles.

First, we drove through Trnovo. Some houses had been bombed, but the town wasn't as damaged as Sarajevo. We saw some police on the streets.

We saw men walking around wearing Chetnik uniforms, but they didn't carry weapons. Part of the peace treaty was that our and their soldiers keep their weapons in the barracks. In Sarajevo, we frequently saw our soldiers in uniform also without weapons. We were frightened and expected someone to stop us, but fortunately nobody did.

We left Trnovo and rode on the open road again. We saw more vehicles and a farmer working on his field wearing a Chetnik uniform.

We drove through Foca. It was less damaged than Trnovo. We saw more men wearing Chetnik uniforms on the streets. We knew that Muslims were "ethnically cleansed" in Foca, and Serbs occupied their homes and owned their property. The Serbs I saw on the street walked around calmly as though nothing had happened.

We rode on the open road again and arrived in Gorazde. The entire city was in ruins. It looked worse than Sarajevo. We saw foreign soldiers on the streets, and they looked Moroccan.

Suad was happy to see us. He said life in Gorazde was very difficult. There was high unemployment. The industries were destroyed. Many people didn't have accommodations. Several relatives were living with Suad's family. The only steady job was with the army.

We attended the ceremony and quickly returned to Hrasnica without incident.

In 1998, we got a letter from the municipality that they wanted to build something else on the spot where my sister's grocery store was, and we had to move. My father and sister went to the municipality to change that decision, but they were unsuccessful. While there, they got more bad news. My sister wouldn't be compensated for her property.

We didn't understand it. Homes and buildings were still damaged from the war. The municipality wasn't repairing them. Why destroy something that's not destroyed?

Mido Botulja, the lawyer who kept Amir and me together in the invalid unit during the war, couldn't help us this time. He had connections with the army but not with the municipality. He was working for an insurance company now.

We got another lawyer, an old man, to try to help us. But there was nothing he could do. The municipality had the legal authority to build roads or buildings, and anything that's in the place where they want to construct has to be removed.

The municipality finally destroyed our store but didn't build anything there. So far, it's an empty lot.

With the destruction of my sister's store, I joined the ranks of the unemployed. In 1999, the unemployment rate in Bosnia was between 35 and 40 percent. Many other veterans were also unemployed, and no relief came to us. We had to pay for everything whether we had a job or not. Usually, the people with jobs had government connections.

I registered with an employment agency and was told that I would have a long wait to get a job. Jobs in Hrasnica were more difficult to get because its industries were destroyed.

Because of my unemployment, I worried constantly and felt

desperate. It also gave me time to think about the peace treaty. This was not the country I fought for. I didn't fight for Bosnia to be separated into two parts. If NATO troops left tomorrow, I would pick up a weapon, attack the Srpska Republic, and make Bosnia one country again. Many of my friends felt the same, especially those who were refugees from the Srpska Republic whose families were killed by the Serbs.

I gave private English lessons to younger people and sold tapestries I made. Friends also helped me.

During this time, I tried to emigrate to America or Canada, but my applications were denied.

Because I spent more time at home, my father and I had more arguments.

Immediately after the end of the war in Bosnia, Kosovars (ethnic Albanians in Kosovo) rebelled against Serbian rule in Kosovo, the former autonomous region of Serbia. They formed the Kosovo Liberation Army (KLA) and began to attack Serbian police units across Kosovo. Milosevic sent in the army and police, and they killed Kosovar civilians as well as KLA members.

In March 1998, the Yugoslavian army and police destroyed Kosovar villages near Pristina, the capital of Kosovo. The KLA grew and seized 40 percent of Kosovo before being defeated by Yugoslavian forces in August 1998. Thousands of Kosovar refugees fled to Albania.

Led by the U.S., NATO sent troops to Albania and Macedonia (areas on the border of Kosovo), and they threatened Milosevic with air strikes and ground attacks unless he removed his troops from Kosovo. The Serbian forces stayed.

Starting on March 24, 1999, NATO aircraft bombed bridges, factories, power stations, and military targets all over Yugoslavia. In response, Serbian troops and police units carried out massive "ethnic cleansing" campaigns in Kosovo in which thousands of Kosovars were killed and thousands more were driven from their homes. Many towns and villages in Kosovo were destroyed.

In the middle of the bombing, two Serbian warplanes entered Bosnia airspace but were shot down before they were able to bomb their targets. I didn't understand it. What targets were there in Bosnia left to bomb? My friends and family thought that Milosevic wanted to widen the war and get the Bosnian Serbs to assist him in fighting NATO. The Bosnian Serbs didn't respond, and it was quiet in Sarajevo and Hrasnica.

After a 78 day NATO bombing campaign and signs that a ground assault was coming, Milosevic agreed to NATO's demands. The Serbian military and police forces withdrew from Kosovo, and NATO troops moved in. KLA units and Kosovar civilians killed and expelled thousands of Serbian civilians in Kosovo in retaliation for Serbian troop actions.

More than 1,500 people were killed in the war in Kosovo, and more than 250,000 became refugees in the end of the war. Most of them were Kosovars.

In December 1999, we heard that Croatian President Franjo Tudjman died. Although no reason was given for his death, it was known he was treated for cancer in 1996. Tudjman was known in Sarajevo for being responsible for "ethnic cleansing" campaigns in Bosnia during the war. However, the UN took no action against him. I felt no satisfaction. Tudjman's death didn't erase the destruction he had brought to Bosnia.

In September 2000, there was another presidential election in Yugoslavia. Milosevic was running against Vojislav Kostunica, a lawyer and leader of an opposition party. Kostunica won the election, but Milosevic refused to recognize the results. Protesters from all over Yugoslavia took to the streets. In Belgrade, they seized the parliament and other government buildings, and Milosevic was forced to step down. My family and I were happy about Milosevic's removal from power but wished it had happened sooner. Much death and destruction could have been avoided.

In October 2000, Alija Izetbegovic resigned from the presidency of Bosnia, citing his age (he was 75) and poor health. I had thought highly of Izetbegovic until he agreed to the division of Bosnia into two separate states. In October 2003, Izetbegovic died from heart disease.

The Kosovo Hospital finally got the necessary equipment to examine my heart, and in 2000, I got a TEE scan. However, the TEE wasn't in the proper condition, and the results of the scan were inconclusive. I was told that a heart operation would be too risky now. As the doctor predicted, my attacks came less often and finally stopped. I still smoke.

Because of arguments with my father, I moved away from my parents' flat in 2000. Now, I live sometimes at a flat in Sarajevo and sometimes at my parents' flat. Because I moved out, I have a better relationship with my father. Before, we constantly had arguments. Now, my father realizes I'm not a small child whom he can tell what he wants. If I don't like what my father does or says, I tell him.

In January 2001, I heard on the radio and TV about complaints against the depleted uranium shells that were dropped by US warplanes on Serbian positions in Bosnia and Kosovo. Uranium waste was coated on US bombs because it could more easily destroy tanks. After the bomb exploded, that waste became a vapor that covered the land and got into the water supply. Other NATO allies raised concerns when some of their soldiers serving in the area contracted leukemia. I remember how happy I felt when NATO finally bombed Serbian positions around Sarajevo. If I had known about the health effects of the depleted uranium then, I wouldn't have been so happy.

In March 2001, Yugoslavian police units stormed Milosevic's Belgrade villa and arrested him. He was delivered to the international War Crimes Tribunal. The current Yugoslavian government was forced to take that action because the US Congress threatened to cut off aid unless they did.

Milosevic faced 66 charges of war crimes in Croatia, Bosnia, and Kosovo. In regard to Bosnia, Milosevic was charged with criminal responsibility for the "widespread killing of thousands of Bosnian Muslims and Bosnian Croats" during the war in Bosnia. The indictment listed execution sites, detention facilities, and locations of more than 8,600 murders across Bosnia. If found guilty of any of those charges, he could face life imprisonment. To those of us who looked at the ruins and destruction that was once our city and our country, no punishment was enough to fit the crime.

I know what happened to most of the people I knew during the war:

My father Ershef Kulin still has the job he had before the war. He works as a clerk for the company, "Forwerding."

My mother Ziza Kulin is unemployed.

My sister Jasmina Granulo works as a shop assistant at another grocery store.

My brother Amir Kulin works the night shift as a security guard at a combination restaurant and motel. His boss sometimes gives him other chores such as cleaning the place. If Amir refuses to do those chores, he'll be fired and unemployed again.

Ferid Mozderac works for "Hydro Jradnja," a construction company. He and his wife are still unable to have a child, and the last time I spoke to him, they hadn't adopted.

Safi lives in Hrasnica with her family. I don't know where she's working. The last time I heard, she was upset because her brother had a kidney transplant, but the operation wasn't successful.

Jepa, my former commander in Siljak, is selling jewelry.

Ramiz Durakovic works as a waiter. He and his wife were divorced. The court gave his wife custody of the children, and they live in Croatia. Ramiz often visits his children there.

Meho Music's bakery was completely destroyed by shells during the war. His son went abroad after the war and helps the family financially. Meho went back to his old job as a taxi driver.

Saba stayed in the army and is a colonel. He married Edisa Muzur, and they have a son. The last time I heard, they were living in a flat in Hrasnica, which was occupied by a Serb who left during the war. They told me that the Serb returned, wanted his flat back, and the court would have to decide that case. I don't know what the court ruled, but judging by the way cases are decided in this matter, Saba and his family probably had to vacate that flat.

When my Serbian neighbor Tomo returned to his flat after the war, Hajra Delic and her sons had to vacate it. They moved to Ilidza. I don't know where Hajra is working. Tomo is looking to sell his flat. He's not living there now but visits occasionally.

I don't know what happened to my former commander Izo in Bijela kosa.

In the middle of 2001, I got a job as a shop assistant for a grocery store called "Agroplod," which is part of a large chain. It's located in the north of Sarajevo and took an hour to get there by tram and bus. I worked there seven days a week and didn't have leisure time. I never met my supervisor and worked with a nice woman named Azra.

I had difficulty with the grocery store job because I wasn't paid regularly, and my employer didn't want to pay for my medical coverage. Because of the insufficient money coming it, I got a part-time job as a waiter. Both of those jobs didn't last long.

In June 2004, I briefly worked as a waiter in a restaurant in Croatia. I got this job partly because they wanted someone who could communicate with the English speaking customers.

Also in June 2004, someone promised to get my friends and me to France if we paid him. We gave him the money, but he disappeared without helping us.

Currently, I work as a receptionist at a pension office. I'm still trying to get to the U.S. or Canada.

Printed in the United States
52772LVS00002B/205

9 781412 048842